Waging

MW01172498

"As a leader in the world of technological innovation, Phil Brattain has worked to bring forward moonshot technologies. He is now tackling a much more difficult and important task—creating a movement for the Moonshot of Universal Love. I applaud Phil for sharing with us his spiritual journey. It is especially important today that we infuse love, empathy, and spirituality into every aspect of our lives. I applaud Phil for encouraging us to engage in a dialogue of how we can bring more love into our lives and into our world."

Sandy Climan, Founder & CEO, Entertainment Media Ventures, Inc.

"Waging Love is a powerful treatise that with clarity and simplicity allows us to align with our innate goodness and become a beacon of LOVE."

James R. Doty, M.D., Founder & Director, Stanford Center for Compassion and Altruism Research and Education (CCARE), New York Times and international bestselling author of *Into the Magic Shop*

"Phil Brattain's WAGING LOVE is a timely message for the world. For a Buddhist, compassion is absolutely essential for one's liberation from suffering, and for one's final enlightenment. And it should be pointed out that compassion in its full meaning—irrespective of how it has been translated in many languages—is one of complete and unadulterated LOVE."

Tenzin N. Tethong, Former Representative of His Holiness the Dalai Lama, and Distringed Fellow, Stanford University

"Universal love is beyond gender and beyond religion. All the great enlightened teachers have taught and expressed universal love, beyond boundaries. Phil Brattain presents this truth through a variety of lenses and compels the reader to experience the power and miracle of universal love within oneself. This is a priceless gift."

Liz Lewinson, Author, *American Buddhist Rebel: The Story of Rama Dr. Frederick Lenz*

"Phil Brattain, author of *Waging Love*, embodies a profound commitment to humanity's transformative journey. His work and character are marked by love and compassion that shines through his exploration of universal consciousness. Phil's vision of a world fueled by universal love and selfless service paints a compelling picture of a future where humanity, collaboratively, creates a world that works for everyone in peace and unconditional love."

Sandra Hanns, Creator and Producer of iGreen Media Group, Co-Founder of Earth Day San Francisco and Licensed Financial Professional

"As an adolescent growing up Catholic, I could never shake the feeling that there is more to this "story," more to our purpose here, and more to each of our spiritual journeys. Having met Phil more than 20 years ago, he continues to be on a relentless pursuit of his own journey of spirituality and enlightenment. In *Waging Love*, Phil shares his collection of studies, observations, and thoughts on why the power of Love is crucial to our survival. As humans, we know that love is powerful – it is the foundation of our most meaningful relationships, and it heals our wounds and pains. It should be no surprise that love is also the power to bridge our divides, helping us embrace the compassion, kindness and empathy required to make us much better participants in this game of life.

The fact that you are reading this means you can hear the phone ringing… now answer the call and start your own transformation."

Mark Besser, Proud Husband, Dad, soon to be Grandfather, Friend, Inquisitive, Aspiring Shaman.

"*Waging Love* is a profound book and compelling vision for transforming our world through the power of unconditional love. Seeing the divine in every person and "waging love" rather than war is a refreshing antidote to the dominating forces of fear, hatred and division. At the heart of *Waging Love* is the most powerful force in the universe—love. After reading this, I want to join the "moonshot" of empowering one billion people over the next decade to channel universal love. I am deeply moved by the vulnerability and sincerity with which Phil shares his own spiritual journey. Anyone seeking to bring more love, unity and understanding into our world should dive into *Waging Love* now."

Declan Dunn, Growth Alchemist, AI Catalyst merging User Generated Content, Community Partnerships and Growth Marketing

"Phil Brattain's exploration of the interconnection between consciousness and the physical universe in *Waging Love* is both intriguing and thought-provoking. His foray into the realms of wave-particle duality, the participatory nature of the universe, and the implications of quantum theory in understanding our reality offers a unique blend of spirituality and science. He challenges conventional notions and invites readers to ponder the profound implications of quantum mechanics in the tapestry of existence. Phil's engagement with quantum mechanics, particularly his examination of concepts like nonlocality, the observer effect, and the nature of consciousness, resonates with the cutting-edge discussions in contemporary physics.

He daringly posits a universe deeply intertwined with human perception, echoing the mystifying and often counterintuitive aspects of quantum theory. This interplay between scientific inquiry and metaphysical speculation exemplifies the ever-evolving nature of our quest to understand the cosmos. *Waging Love* not only contributes to this discourse but also exemplifies the potential of interdisciplinary approaches in unraveling the mysteries of our universe."

Joshua May, Board Member & Chief Engineer—MW Enterprises LLC

Waging Love

Waging Love

How to Transform Our World
One Heart at a Time

PHIL BRATTAIN

Published by Miracle Moonshot Media
www.waging.love

ISBN (paperback): 979-8-89269-361-5
ISBN (ebook): 979-8-89269-362-2

Book design and production by www.AuthorSuccess.com

To the LORD of LOVE
And His Bride
Humanity Forever Transformed
Past, Present, and Future
With No One and Nothing Ever Lost

CONTENTS

God Is Love

Hidden near the end of the New Testament in a little-known letter by Saint John "the Divine" (1 John) is a three-word phrase that has far more power than any nuclear arsenal. Only this is a creative force, much like that which gave rise to the Universe. "**God IS Love.**" (1 John 4:8)

It doesn't merely say that God is "loving." Rather, God IS Love. If God IS Love, then **Love IS God**. *Pure Love, Divine Love, Sacred Love.* This is the Love that conquered the Roman Empire. This very same Love will transform our world into the legendary paradise of the millennium. Just one heart at a time. That is enough.

Above the raw survival needs of air, water, food, shelter, safety, and security, you desire Love. Most likely, you learned somewhere in your childhood that this love is conditional, scarce, and in short supply. You can never get enough. You've got to hold onto it for dear life.

The Christian narrative points us to the **Lord of Love**, Jesus Christ, the Chosen One. Clearly, this man did what no man before Him did. Jesus took upon Himself the karma of the whole world; past, present, and future. He owned our world out of an Infinite Love that stretches out across history and transforms it. Christ made Love the currency of the New Humanity, the New Divinity.

I have heard His Inner Voice many times. It is the Voice of pure love beyond comprehension, more like that of a mother, or even a lover. I have learned that as we commune with Him, as we invoke His Living

Presence, that miraculous Love flows right through us and transforms everyone around us. I know the limits of my love. I have no illusion it can even compare with His Love. However, **I can see no limits to THAT LOVE.** Love is a feeling you can never fake. It is also a state of being that gives you license to accomplish the impossible. *That Love is the ultimate miracle.*

This book, *Waging Love*, is written so that you may discover that Love for yourself. It points to direct access to Universal Love. *Anytime. Anywhere.* Not only that, *Waging Love* points to the possibility of your channeling Universal Love towards anyone or anything. *Anytime. Anywhere.* From there, it offers you an open invitation to join the *Moonshot* of our lives. **In the next ten years, we can impact one billion people around this planet, empowering them with direct access to this Love and the ability to direct that Love to anyone at any time.**

I welcome you to join me on this journey. I am deeply honored by your participation. By the boundless Grace of God, we will all make it together!

Phil Brattain
Poet. Prophet. Mystic.

Belmont, California
September 23, 2023

Foreword

Since meeting one another at the New Living Expo in San Francisco in the Spring of 2016, Phil and I have been engaged in an ongoing conversation about the nature of reality and truth. From plumbing the depths of human depravity and imperfections (commonly known as talking about politics, war, disease, crime and destruction), we invariably end up high on some mountain top surveying the human condition itself.

What do, and can, we know, and what are the limits of our potential to change the world for good?

After a lengthy discourse, I invariably ask myself, from such low and unpromising beginnings how did we end UP here...again...and again?

Waging Love provides the answer to those essential questions and to so much more. It points to Phil's unfailing optimism and firm foundation of faith, driven by unshakeable understandings and personal verifications that we are all God's children. As such, we are destined to succeed, beyond the slightest shadow of a doubt, in The Great and the Good, whatever that may be and however dimly we perceive it.

Not only that. We do not even need to be good to get started. Sinners, scamps and scoundrels are welcome. In fact, no one, not a single soul, is excluded. Even the worst most heinous villains can join in. Indeed, we should include our enemies most especially since the very subjects of our own particular grievances and brand of anger lead us to the ground of our illusions and, paradoxically, to peace. For when we can learn to dissolve hatred and judgement, Phil would encourage us to know, we can truly open our hearts to Heaven's unremitting glory and become a beacon of light.

The answer to so many complex problems it seems, therefore, is quite simple. There is a door to which there is a key.

So, imagine yourself deep in conversation with Phil, bemoaning the state of the world and the sufferings of the people in it, then entertain this thought just for one moment:

Your potential to effect positive change is limitless, informed by the power of Love

What objections might you have to this statement and how would you question its veracity? Are you filled with offense at its naivety or presumption? Do your own convictions point you to quite different conclusions? Or, are you just a tiny bit curious? Even if you wish to respond with this challenge, "NONSENSE! COME ON THEN, SHOW ME HOW THAT CAN BE TRUE", then *Waging Love* is for you.

Above all, this book is an invitation to engage in a profound discourse (with yourself). You are already standing at the threshold. Find the key, turn the lock, and step in...

Michael Bishop
Poet, Mystic, Sceptic, and Writer / Editor at large

More Power Than You Could Possibly Imagine

Thank you for opening up this book. You are about to discover who you truly are. Despite all your doubts and fears, you are utterly magnificent, a son or daughter of the living God! Your mandate is to become an avatar, a bodhisattva, a messiah. For many of us, that means becoming Christ, becoming God.

While you may not even remotely feel this of yourself, *you have the power within you to transform our world by continuously transforming yourself.* This can emerge as a spontaneous process. You will ultimately find that you can *move, touch,* and *inspire* everyone you encounter by continuously presencing God as Love. You will begin to see God in more and more people. Eventually, you will discover God even in yourself.

Why Share This with You?

In my professional life, I offer corporate and business development at the executive level for startups, often required by foreign nationals seeking a position in the North American market out of San Francisco's Silicon Valley. Although born in America, I am very close to the South Asian diaspora here and across the USA. I have gained priceless insights from daily interacting with international engineers and entrepreneurs who have an entirely different cultural and spiritual outlook. This experience opened me up to a global spiritual perspective.

I co-authored *Awaken Perfection: The Journey of Conscious Revelation* (*www.awakenperfection.com*) with Audrone Wippich. We were graciously endorsed by the grandson of the Mahatma, Dr. Arun Gandhi, and the president of the Dalai Lama Foundation, Tenzin N. Tethong. In that book, we offered a fresh vision of planetary, or universal, consciousness; a consciousness that changes everything. *Awaken Perfection* serves as a guide to thriving in a radically transformed landscape.

I also wrote 200 articles for the web magazine, *Conscious Owl*, addressing a full range of issues in contemporary global spirituality. Audrone and I attracted a number of devoted readers who found the content inspirational.

Why Love?

In the wake of our initial efforts to convey this mission, vision, and message, it became increasingly clear that Divine Love is the entry point. Everyone wants more and more love in their life, but few know how to gain direct access on a continuous basis. While a good number of us realize love is spiritual in nature, far too many of us grew up believing in an angry, disgruntled God smoking a pipe on a rocking chair, high in the heavens, capriciously throwing thunderbolts down on us.

Even when the Love of Christ was willingly shared by evangelicals, the message was all too often undermined by an unconscious preoccupation with hell. If you don't accept this offer, you will be condemned to eternal punishment, gnashing your teeth in the total absence of His presence and His Love.

Precious few clergy would ever stand up to them and remind us that this bankrupt theology was far from the norm in original Christianity. A good number of the early Church Fathers were Universalists who believed that even Satan would ultimately be redeemed.

In recent years, scientific, technological, and philosophic knowledge has vastly expanded with the mobile internet. In major metropolitan areas, you can now meet people from any race, nationality, ethnicity, or religion. With enough diligence, it is possible to get to the truth behind it all through persistent conversation, contemplation, and scholarship.

I have had the opportunity to live and work in a region of the world continuously reinventing the future, surrounded by accomplished professionals much richer, more handsome, smarter, and younger than I. If you saw me on the street, you would most likely walk right past me.

However, deep within myself, I have something you might give anything to own: The full realization of GOD as LOVE. Does the Universe have our back? One dose of this ambrosia, and you will answer in the affirmative.

Divine Love, Universal Love, the Love Christ demonstrated on the cross, is the most powerful force in all the universe. It can raise the dead and grant you eternal life. By drinking deeply of that Love, you will BECOME God. As God IS Love, so will you be.

At the pinnacle of their spectacular career, the Beatles declared to all the world, "All you need is LOVE!"

They sang this live to the world for the very first time on a satellite television broadcast simultaneously around the planet. While the Beatles could indulge every aspiration, only one thing truly mattered.

Why Christianity?

You can be of any faith, or none. God only looks at your heart. However, Christianity, of all the great spiritual traditions, does bet everything on divine love. It is all about continuously communing with the ultimate incarnation of that Love, Jesus Christ.

I say this without reservation, having studied the world's great religious traditions for over twenty years. They all offer the golden rule and enjoin you to love your neighbor. However, few of them urge you to love your enemy and bless those who curse you. Those practitioners who do become like Saint Francis, Mahatma Gandhi, or the Dalai Lama.

Waging Love will introduce you to Universal Consciousness, Universal Love, and Universal Presence. It will profile practices that can make all of this very real to you. For example, if you systematically bless everyone

3

and everything, you will not stay the same person for long. You will be transformed into the highest possible version of yourself in this very lifetime; the divine being you truly are!

Why Traditional Language?

In *Waging Love*, I address God in traditional terms, using the male gender. This is because the traditional usage still carries the greatest emotional weight. In truth, God is both male and female, and transpersonal, beyond male or female. God does not favor any one race, nationality, or ethnicity over any other, because God is within each and every one of us.

Gender issues subside when we become conscious that God is our ultimate Lover. God adores us. He is totally in love with us. He lives in us, through us, as us. We find ourselves irreversibly in a LOVE STORY. Given the LORD of LOVE is the morning star, each one of us presencing Him becomes a divine lover along with Him.

While many other more meaningful terms can be used for God, such as Higher Power, Infinite Intelligence, the Transcendent Mystery, or the Supreme Identity, none have the emotional impact of "GOD," which is ultimately derived from the English word, "good." In this book, "God" is a welcome and necessary placeholder for our Source, our Creator, our only True and Ultimate Self.

Why Not Now?

In moving forward, you have much more to gain than you could possibly lose. In reading *Waging Love*, you discover both who you are and why you're here. You will be given the context to see the world and your life in a daring new way. Much like a caterpillar morphing into a butterfly, you will be given the wings to fly. The higher you go, the more of God you will see. Your divine nature will suddenly become fully available to you.

Our world today is challenged as never before as every single human institution breaks down and undergoes transformation. While creation is inherently abundant, hundreds of millions of us go through life accepting severe limitation. Hunger, epidemics, terrorism, and environmental stress seem constant companions. Worst of all, many of us suffer a spiritual emptiness that makes life all but absurd.

Only one thing will make the difference, and you can wake everyone you meet up to that difference. It is the **Infinite and Absolute Love** hiding just below the surface. As you do your part, the flame will spread from one person to another all around the planet. You will gain a mission, vision and message that will make your divine talent a gift to us all. You will be in line to realize all that you were meant to be.

Thank you for joining us!

PART 1

Universal Consciousness

The Resurrecting Power of the Love of Christ is Absolute. There Are No Limitations.

We are immersed in an ocean of Love on the perfect planet in the perfect solar system in the perfect galaxy. This Love is the source of all life. In this Love, we move and breathe and have our being. This LOVE IS GOD, and GOD IS THIS LOVE.

We live in a glorious Love story. This story stars the Lord of Love, the once and future king. This king was revealed to display the full force of divine Love. Every actor interacts with every other, each story intermeshes with all the others. Yet always there is only ONE of us.

The Christian good news is truly *glorious news*. The king who died and is risen lies within every one of us. We all have a birthright of direct access to this Love. We are free to channel this Love to anyone or anything at any time. This Love has resurrecting power. It is absolute. No one and nothing can possibly overcome it. It blows away any and all limitations.

CHAPTER ONE

Ultimate Moonshot: One Billion of Us Together Sharing Universal Love

In the mid-twentieth century, a stunning race began between America and the former Soviet Union. Russia led with the first satellite, Sputnik, and the first man to orbit the earth, Cosmonaut Yuri Gagarin. In May 25, 1961, America jumped into the race as well with a commitment to land a man on the moon before that decade was over. Both nations devoted massive amounts of time, energy, and capital to accomplish the seemingly impossible. Finally, *American Astronaut, Neil Armstrong, first stepped onto the moon on July 20, 1969.*

While our space program led by NASA has since floundered, three billionaires have taken huge steps to revive it as a commercial endeavor: Elon Musk, Jeff Bezos, and Richard Branson. They have created their own rockets and spacecraft from scratch and successfully entered near space. Elon Musk's Space X has succeeded in launching orbital flights with astronauts aboard to serve the International Space Station. *Musk's vowed mission is, not only to return to the Moon, but to colonize Mars so that humanity has a backup home in the Universe.*

More important than even landing on Mars is a new mission to establish Universal Love among humanity within the next decade. This can give humanity time to heal its many divisions and conflicts, including endless wars, random terrorism, environmental stress, and economic volatility. It has become increasingly apparent that this mission must be *spiritual in nature. An inner technology is being developed that embraces and extends the insights from the great spiritual traditions of humanity. How to access and channel this technology to love everyone and everything is our breakthrough.*

The Moonshot of Universal Love

A moonshot of Universal Love will empower one billion of us over the next ten years to directly access and channel *Infinite, Unconditional Love at any time* towards *anyone* under *any conditions.* Initially, this entails mastering this extraordinary love, so that you can be in a place to meaningfully share it with other people.

Once individuals gain direct access to this love and begin to channel it to others, they will endeavor to share it with everyone they encounter. They will have the means to regularly review the context and practice the techniques that evoke this sacred presence.

The moonshot demands leveraging digital networks and media to impact as many people as possible all around the world. As the movement grows, *new technologies will emerge to sufficiently accelerate the number of practitioners to reach critical mass,* when the process develops a momentum of its own.

Universal Love—the Ultimate Moonshot

Universal Love will give us the time we need to accomplish *any other* moonshot, such as setting up a permanent colony on Mars. This Love is a prerequisite to sustaining a civilization of complex, multiplanetary beings. It will boost the level of global cooperation higher than previously imagined. The consideration and sensitivity of the practitioners will inspire any number of ingenious global initiatives.

This Love gives everyone what they need most once their bare survival needs are met. It entails profound respect, appreciation, and admiration for every person with *a growing realization of the sacredness of life.* Sharing, giving, and participation will become spontaneous as the illusion of separation between us gradually dissolves.

This Love is essential to harmonizing the diverse challenges and needs facing global society. Over the millennia, we have developed alternative narratives on why we are here, where we should go and what is most important, as codified in the great spiritual traditions. We will soon develop a common language that can unpack these fascinating world-views and integrate them into a vastly expanded perspective.

How I Opened Up to Universal Love

In October 2013, I was going nowhere fast. I was stretched just to make ends meet. Earlier, an offshore client, after several months of steady work, refused to pay me a dime. More and more, I felt all alone. While my tiny studio was in an upscale neighborhood, I had no covered parking, no storage, and no view besides the fence of a neighboring apartment. A bookcase in front of my bed was my only privacy from people peering through the sliding glass door. The tiny space was so crowded I had to make my way without stumbling between boxes with a creaky old couch dominating the front area. My saving grace was a private office near the water, where I could breathe easier and appear normal.

Earlier I had been diagnosed with serious blood sugar issues. I thus carefully watched my diet. Having delayed seeing a podiatrist on a slight cut in my little toe, my entire left ankle was now swollen. I knew I had to go see him immediately. When I arrived at his office, the doctor expressed visible concern. After careful inspection, he immediately directed me to a surgeon at a nearby hospital. I was totally unprepared for something like this, very nervous. I made up my mind to do whatever I had to do.

When I met with the surgeon, he confirmed that one of my toes had become gangrene—I needed an immediate operation. With neither social security nor health insurance, I was in an awkward position. I had not bothered to ask any simple questions, such as the cost or the recovery period. I called my two closest friends, one of whom joined me at the hospital. After an intense discussion, I felt that I had no other choice. I made peace with myself to sign my left little toe away.

The actual procedure was disarmingly simple. I was wheeled into the operating room and heavily sedated. They then wheeled me up to what turned out to be a lovely private room with a view. They were deeply concerned that the infection might spread all over. Maybe I would lose my left leg, or even die! I could steal sleep for only an hour or two before being interrupted by needles. When morning came, I woke up to see an air suction device attached to my left ankle to mitigate the bleeding.

What totally surprised me were the feelings spontaneously arising within me of profound gratitude and love for the physicians and nurses. I was getting more and more attention, something lacking in my life. I was able to call friends from my iPhone and use my iPad to access the Web. My two closest friends visited me multiple times, gladly doing errands for me. My closest female friend, Audrone, took my car and drove it back home. I had given her my keys. She faithfully checked the mail and kept me up to date.

Before I realized it, I had an office setup on my hospital bed, and could work my part-time job to my client's satisfaction. After various other friends visited me, I no longer felt alone. When they left, I went through Neale Donald Walsch's *Conversations with God* trilogy. In studying Neale's experience, I began to have my own two-way discussions with God, a still small voice of infinite love and compassion.

On the final day, everything worked like a clock. Audrone was right there with my car. We got all my personal possessions out of the hospital. I noticed how stunningly beautiful everything was outside. When we got back to my studio, I thought I had entered the wrong door. Everything was in perfect shape. The clumsy couch had been pulled outside. The carpets were whisper clean, the furniture waxed, the kitchen floor immaculate! I had my iMac for TV, my iPad for entertainment and my MacBook Pro for work. Best of all, Audrone would be my part-time companion for the next two months.

I came to realize that losing my left little toe held a hidden blessing. In dealing with a seemingly impossible situation, I opened myself up to a whole new world I would otherwise never have seen. So many people cared for me through unselfish acts of kindness. I gradually began to open up to Universal Love.

What Universal Love Will Look Like

People all over the world will keep outdoing themselves with consideration of others without the slightest need to justify or defend themselves. The more you see God in every person, the less concern you will have over being abused. You will want to help them realize the highest possible version of themselves in this lifetime.

We will realize that enlightenment and empowerment are our inalienable birthright. Educational curricula will finally promote and encourage spiritual, as much as social, economic, and political development. The religious wars, and the terrorism associated with them, will become a thing of the past.

We will commit ourselves to a world that works for everyone with *no one*, and *nothing*, left out. Realizing that we are the source of our own experience and children of the Living God, we will no longer consider poverty, disease, and oppression as *their* problems. We will be accountable for co-creating it. We will finally see Planet Earth as the astronauts and cosmonauts see it, with *no frames* and *no boundaries*.

We will take much greater joy in the accomplishments of others than those of our own. All players in the Big Game will consider *they succeed only, and if, you succeed*. It will be a race to honor and serve everyone else. The Gift Economy envisioned in the Burning Man festival will become a daring new standard for humanity.

What Makes the Moonshot of Universal Love Possible

A revolution in transportation and communications has emerged that makes the seemingly impossible feasible. From roads to waterways to air routes to space exploration. From print to telegraph to telephone to computer. Mobile digital media now enable us to *move, touch*, and *inspire* anyone else on earth in real time.

We can now speak freely to global citizens of any language through automatic translation. This is no longer restricted to the translators at the United Nations or to the intelligence community or even to the jetsetters. Our smartphones will increasingly have translation built in. The Silicon Valley search company, Google, has already gone far in this direction.

More and more people crave that which lies just beyond their basic survival needs. Against all appearances, overall prosperity and a broader distribution of wealth are actually *increasing* among nations. Standards of living are on the uptick, despite economic volatility and monetary instability. People everywhere are placing a higher value on the intangibles of life.

The New Paradigm That Will Change Everything

While the planets still revolve around the stars and the stars around the galaxy, they all lie as much within the context of our own Absolute Being as we lie within them. Matter is better viewed as conscious energy. Not a "thing," our Universe is the vibrant expression of Pure Spirit.

We are all sons and daughters of the Living God. We share with our Source intelligence, imagination, and compassion. We are tuning into the power of Spirit. We are becoming comfortable with the idea that behind the vast expanse of forms resides pure *Being, Consciousness,* and *Bliss,* or put in Western terms, pure Light, Life, and Love. *Humanity is inherently and inviolably spiritual.*

We have infinite power at our disposal through Universal Love, which no one and nothing can possibly overcome. While this Love is much more subtle than overt, it is vastly more effective. It works from within. *People have no defense against pure love since this is what each of us wants most.* Nuclear weapons can, indeed, perpetrate mass destruction, but *Love has the creative power to not only give each of us birth, but to create whole new worlds.*

Why the Way of Love Is All We Need

As Christ put it, "Seek first the Kingdom of God, and His righteousness, and all these things shall be added unto you." (Matthew 6:33) The Way of Love, as opposed to Contemplation or Knowledge, is how most of humanity finds God. When you embody Love, people see God in you. They interact with you as someone sacred or holy, much like a saint.

The Kingdom of God is Divine Love, the "Pearl of Great Price," which everyone, everywhere seeks throughout their lives. Christ was the first in the West to come out with a "new world order." He taught us all to see the Creator as our Loving Father. Our true wealth lies in service to people everywhere, whether friend, neighbor, or enemy. This results in the fruit of Christ Consciousness: *Love, Joy,* and *Peace.*

When you love others first, they are often moved to love you back in spades. While most of us only occasionally come from service, those who consistently provide it make a massive difference. This service is seen in concrete action, but even more in a profound loving regard for others.

How We Can Go from Fear and Hatred to Faith and Love

Deliberately seek out communities, networks, and media focused on faith and love, rather than those focused on fear and hatred. During the recent global pandemic, we have seen various levels of government act oppressively. The mass media became focused entirely on systematically blaming anyone else but themselves, as they did with President Trump. The Bill of Rights was too often disregarded throughout America, and the voters, themselves, were figuratively muzzled.

Fear and hatred are disempowering emotions with very low vibration. They appeal to bare survival and have no room for faith in God or faith in the goodness of humanity. People must be separated from one another by the "new normal." This is especially dangerous when the mass media reach a consensus and begin active censorship. It sets the stage for a technological, totalitarian surveillance state.

Faith and love are empowering emotions with high vibration. They inspire people to greatness, to live in possibility and look within themselves for ways we can build a better world. You feel energized in a meeting with this kind of ambience. Suddenly, life is worth living.

The more you focus on faith and Love, the more that energy will feel right to you. You will begin to see alternatives to those large institutions that portray victimhood, as the mainstream mass media so often do. You will either disengage with those entities or consciously enter them as a change agent. Gradually people caught up in no-win games will come to you to explore fresh possibilities.

How Joining This Moonshot Will Transform Your Life

We all find our ultimate fulfillment in embracing a cause greater than ourselves. After World War II, visionary world citizens created the United Nations. During the Cold War, President Kennedy organized the Peace Corps. When the U.S. economy was languishing, President Clinton with the help of his technologically astute Vice President, Al Gore, successfully commercialized the Internet with full cooperation from Silicon Valley.

As you give the world what it needs most, opportunities will open to you everywhere. When you can regularly access and channel divine love *to anyone at any time under any conditions*, you will impact people in the most positive way possible. It will be more a matter of your BEING, than your DOING. *The more you start being there for others, the more you will start doing the right thing.*

Given the magnitude of this mission, it will bring out the heroic in you, deeply inspiring others. The more you truly love people, the more their issues will become your issues. You will stop buying into apparent limitations. It will become much easier for you to do outrageous things. Back in the 1980s, the dynamic Chicago preacher and community organizer, Jesse Jackson, freed prisoners in various countries as a citizen diplomat. Before him, no one even thought this might be possible. Just leave it all up to the politicians.

As you experience great delight in the transformation of others, you will enjoy an endless source of fulfillment. Few things are as glorious as turning people from fear to faith and hatred to love. You will start to look for the highest possibility of the people in your world. You will begin to incarnate God in such a way as to astound people who underestimated your potential.

How You Can Make a Difference with This Moonshot

You, yourself, offer a unique combination of talent, ideas, and connections required to realize so great a moonshot. When you awaken to your Divine Self, you will find yourself vastly more powerful than you ever imagined. *It takes only one person to start a revolution.* After the end of World War II, the test pilot, Chuck Yeager, broke the sound barrier. Within twenty years, humanity went to the moon. Back in the 1970s, Steve Jobs and Bill Gates dreamt of a PC on every desk. Now we find a smart-phone in every pocket.

When you continuously focus on God *as Love,* you will find yourself living on a higher plane. While hundreds of millions fear God as a crazy tyrant in a rocking chair throwing thunderbolts down on a bewildered humanity, millions upon millions still realize God as *their very best friend who will always have their back.*

You will gradually become, like Christ, St. Francis and Gandhi, the Greatest Lover in *your* world, as nothing can match the glory of Universal, or Divine Love. Jesus Christ, St. Francis, and Mahatma Gandhi were real people born into a world constrained by unique predicaments. With Christ, it was Roman oppression of the Holy Land. With St. Francis, it was the futile crusades. With Gandhi, it was British exploitation of India. In every case, they gave people back their freedom, *beginning from within.*

Why Now Is the Perfect Time to Start

Since action always begins in the present, it is never too early to start transforming the quality of your life, as well as that of everyone else. No task is more urgent. Humanity must increase its love for God, for the world, and for one another by an order of magnitude if we are to pass our final exam of developing a sane, sustainable, and nurturing civilization.

17

While greater and greater affluence is emerging in unexpected parts of the world, such as Asia Pacific, people there are realizing there is more to life. Once you have all your survival needs met, you begin to seek the spiritual. Wealth by itself never guarantees love, joy, and peace.

Since this may well be the greatest opportunity in your lifetime, *why wait?* If you feel the call, invite your friends, family, and community to make a difference. In his youth, Chad Pregracken was distressed at all the junk he saw in the Mississippi river. He organized community action and in 2013 became CNN's *Person of the year.*

When you directly connect and commune with the Source of Universal Love, you will experientially discover Who you are as Pure Love, more than equal to any challenge ahead. Think of all the times you dreamt of doing something, in the words of Steve jobs, "insanely great." *What if you move forward, even if you make a ton of mistakes? What if now you have infinite power at your disposal through Divine Love?*

Remember:

- The technological infrastructure necessary to give one billion of us over the coming decade direct access to Universal Love, and the ability to channel that Love to anyone, anywhere, at any time is fully deployed.

- The inner technology required to rapidly catalyze unconditional love among all people has been abstracted from our great spiritual traditions.

- A global sacred, but nonsectarian, movement is emerging that will inform and train people everywhere with this inner technology.

CHAPTER TWO

The New Paradigm: Only God

In the decades leading up to the latest global pandemic, a whole new view of reality has emerged due to a dramatically different perspective that contemporary scientists have constructed of our world. It suggests that the Universe we see all around us is ultimately a projection, an interplay of our own consciousness.

This shift in thinking is even greater than that which triggered the Renaissance and the modern view of life. In the Middle Ages, it was widely held that the sun and planets floated in crystalline spheres above our flat planet. We were small specks of protoplasm of no ultimate consequence.

The new view has the world around us appear less and less solid. It is as much in us as we are in it. Over hundreds of years, humanity has yet to discover the smallest particle or the furthest star. It is becoming virtually certain that we play out our lives in the mind of God.

5MeO DMT

In recent decades, pioneers in psychedelics discovered a natural substance more potent than LSD. It comes from the glands of the Sonoran toad in the Southwestern United States and Mexico. A secretion is crystalized and then smoked. The key substance is a type of DMT referred to as 5MeO. The smoke is so potent that experimenters often experience "God" within, not hours or minutes, but seconds. Research indicates this is a natural substance that powerfully impacts our nervous system.

At the climax of the experience, they realize that there is only Infinite Light. Nothing can be found outside of that Light. There is only God.

Smokers need not be religious. "God" is the only word that can convey the magnitude of that impact. After fifteen or twenty minutes, the experience subsides. However, the smokers ever after are spiritual, as if undergoing a life-altering near-death experience (NDE).

Observer / Observed / Observation

In various forms of deep meditation, or *samadhi*, practitioners gradually go beyond being the observer. They begin to identify with that which they observe. This results in their becoming that which they observe, whether a candle, a mandala, or a mantra.

Eventually, they come to identify with the process of observation itself. They realize they are both the observer and that which they observe. Meditation becomes a matter of sitting and becoming aware of awareness itself.

Ultimately, meditators realize that they are both all of it—observer, observation, and process of observation—and none of it—neither observer, nor observation, nor the process of observation itself. They are just being. As the Indian Vedanta puts it, "Sat | Chit | Ananda," or "Being | Consciousness | Bliss."

Wave / Particle Duality

Early physicists debated endlessly whether light functions more as a wave or a particle. At first, light seemed quite naturally a wave, as it spreads out to fill whatever space is available. Later, as experiments progressed, discrete particle-like attributes were detected, which they referred to as *quanta*.

Since the particles were individually detectible, the hardcore insisted that light was reducible to particles. They weren't certain how to account for their wave-like nature. So, they dubbed them "wavicles."

Eventually, the waves were held to be probability waves. At any one place, it was more probable that a particle might occur than at another place. Given this understanding, one wonders just how real *anything* can be.

Goldilocks Principle

Astrophysicists have identified several dozen preconditions essential to the formation of life. It appears that, in our galaxy, our Earth is uniquely placed in relation to the sun, not too close and not too far. If too close to the sun, it would be too hot for life and water would evaporate. One only needs to think of a planet like Venus.

Also, our planet has enough carbon dioxide to generate carbon-based life forms. Our atmosphere is a mixture of gases, including nitrogen, oxygen, and carbon dioxide. Plants consume carbon dioxide and release oxygen, which animal life totally depends upon.

Our atmosphere contains sufficient hydrogen and oxygen for the formation of water. Water, in the form of the ocean, gives the bluish tint to our atmosphere.

Given the other planets in our solar system don't enjoy this unique combination, they are much less favorable for the formation of life. This formation, like the fairy tale character, Goldilocks, seems so extremely favorable as to be necessarily designed by the Creator.

Interbeing

Thich Nhat Hanh, the Nobel Peace Prize recipient, coined the phrase "interbeing" to capture how everything and everyone is related to everything and everyone else. In India, this was traditionally referred to as *Indra's Net*, where everywhere we behold an infinite strand of pearls, where every pearl reflects every other pearl. We can't have a body to move around without a world to support it.

Each of us can be seen as unique only with others with whom to compare. Every person is necessary to every other person. Each of our perceptions is intermeshed with all the others, as if to form a world.

Without an observer, neither body nor world would exist. This goes not just for humans, but also for plants and animals. We are all one because everything contains everything else.

Nonlocality

Albert Einstein was never happy with quantum theory as it developed. He grew up in what he thought was a deterministic universe, where there were no accidents. In trying to disprove quantum theory, Einstein proposed, as a thought experiment, that if two particles are paired together and then infinitely separated, their spins would have to continue to be correlated.

His challenge was taken on seriously by the community of physicists. One physicist, John Bell, mathematically made the case for nonlocality, that you could pair two particles and then separate them to the other side of the universe. As far as they went, they would still maintain their spins in parallel.

Later, rigorous experiments demonstrated that nonlocality is, indeed, real. The two separated particles "know" how each other will spin, while maintaining vast distances that would exceed the speed of light. This put in question Einstein's celebrated use of light as a constant; the highest velocity thought possible at 186,282 miles per second.

Dark Matter / Dark Energy

Astronomers discovered that space is expanding and even accelerating. This was observable in large telescopes, something even Einstein had to admit. The implications upset the existing model of the universe. To explain this, astrophysicists adopted the notion of invisible matter and energy.

According to the new cosmology, most of the actual matter and energy is "dark matter" and "dark energy," with visible matter and energy but a fraction of the total. This suggests that we are in for a whole new paradigm of the universe.

This very recent theory is still being developed with the aid of powerful new space telescopes. It is continually being refined. It might be possible that the external universe is an expression of infinite consciousness. As one great astrophysicist, Sir James Jeans, put it, "The universe begins to look more like a great thought than a great machine."

No Smallest Particle

As physics progressed in the last century or two, the smallest particle moved from the atom to the subatomic particle. The whole notion of billiard balls with electrons flying around them began to be described as clouds of energy. In particle accelerators, what was once considered an uncuttable solid was now proven to be breakable.

The more powerful the electronic microscope, the more particles we can see. The greater the accelerator, the more subatomic particles appear out of nowhere. We never see the void, or no more particles.

The more powerful the radio telescope, the more stars we see. We never see a pure blank. There are always more and more stars. From a philosophic perspective, we well might ask, "Are our acts of observation, themselves, actually creating the particles and stars that we see?"

Participatory Universe

The great American physicist, John Wheeler, introduced the concept of "participatory universe" to explain how neither the observer, nor the observed, are independent of each other. The human observer, and the universe she observes, are so interrelated that you cannot have one without the other. No observer, no universe. No universe, no observer.

John Wheeler was close to a philosophic idealist who believed that our observations literally "create" the universe. Our observations are an experience of interrelatedness. The universe is our playground, which we create as we go along. We create it, just as it creates us.

The universe thus created conforms to the requirements of the individual observer. The universe you see is your own interpretation, while the "real" universe isn't really out there. It is all a play of consciousness.

Galaxies Spin Within

If there is only "God," then all the galaxies spin within the context of our own absolute being. All that we see is within our one and only true Self. The universe, independent from us, is not really out there. There is only whom and what we call God.

We can think of our body with the surrounding community as our small self, who we pretend to be most of the time. It dances away its life within the world of form. Our individual self is a uniquely precious localization of God. God is appearing as you and me in the Kingdom of Heaven.

Our true Self is both beyond, and includes, the world of form, as well as our body. The more conscious we become, the more we see only God, even in the light post and the highway. When we come home to God, we can transform the world we experience into a Garden of Eden.

Remember

- There is only God. Each and every one of us is a uniquely precious localization of our ultimate Self.

- We live in God's dream, and who and what we call "God" is our only true Self.

- We co-create our universe with God moment by moment. Everyone we meet is but our other Self.

CHAPTER THREE

Avatar Outlook:
100% Responsibility

As the new paradigm in physics gets established, it becomes most apparent that we all share a fundamental responsibility, as no one is definitively "out there" to perpetrate the crimes of which we accuse others. Our bodies are as real as theirs, but not more real. It is more like a mutual dance on a movie screen.

As we discover the dreamlike nature of our lives, and how we live out a story, it is possible to awaken to the nature of that story, that it is a divine love story. Somehow, we are both watching it and playing it out. As we become conscious of the process, we can shape the outcome and contribute to the masterpiece.

Responsibility is always a choice. While it may initially appear as an imposition, those of us who choose to approach our lives from the vantage point of Source discover an overwhelming sense of empowerment. We discover our only true and ultimate identity in the process.

From Victimization to Empowerment

Victimization is inevitable when you deflect responsibility; empowerment is inevitable when you assume responsibility. Most of the world suffers from one form or another of victimization. To stand out, to make a difference, the price is to give up forever the option of playing victim.

Leadership requires the assumption of responsibility. Since so few people are comfortable doing this, true leaders always stand out as people you can count on. Thus, they often receive more rewards than the general public.

Responsibility leads to freedom. When people realize they are no longer being blamed, they quickly open up. Someone has to initiate this. Why not let it be you?

No One "Out There" to Blame

The new physics reveals that whom or what you blame is not actually "out there." Everyone and everything you see is actually within the context of our own absolute being. God, or the universe, is localized through you. Blame, shame, and guilt are expressions of ignorance.

The people you come across mirror what is happening within you. When you blame them, you find you are only blaming yourself. You will find no satisfaction or fulfillment in doing so.

The more you help others, the more they will help you and recognize you as a true leader. Increasingly, individual or collective irresponsibility will no longer appeal to you in any way, shape, or form.

Source Your Own Experience

As you are continually experiencing moment by moment, source that very experience. Realize that whatever you think, feel, or do is just that. A thought is just a thought, a feeling is just a feeling, an action is just an action. They need not mean anything.

Shift your attention from what is happening outside as being independent of you, to what is going on within you. For action to be effective, you need to look in the right direction . . . within.

You will find that you are no longer fooled by appearances. Appearances are always just that, appearances. You look within to find what is real.

Simple Acknowledgement

Responsibility entails a simple acknowledgment that you are the source of your own experience. This includes what you do to others, what others do to you, and what others do to others, even around the planet. It is all YOUR world.

Our judgments, evaluations, conclusions, and decisions, as well as our considerations, are all what we add to our pure experience. Again, a judgment is just that: a judgment. An evaluation is just that: an evaluation. A conclusion is just that: a conclusion; and a decision is just that: a decision.

The more you own your own experience, the freer you become. You give up the habit of continually excusing yourself. You did what you did. You felt what you felt. Others did what they did. Others felt what they felt. No causality is implied.

Willingness to Come from Source

When you come from a higher perspective, you feel no need to judge others. You can act responsibly, even when you don't see how you possibly could have caused it. For example, you hear of a war on the other side of the ocean. You no longer consider them a pack of fools. They are just players in a cosmic game.

Whatever someone else says or does to you is what occurred to them in the moment. Somehow you created it. When you give up blame, you can respond much more creatively.

When you realize that who you truly are is everyone and everything, then what another does to another on the other side of the planet is not THEIR problem, it is YOUR problem.

Opportunity, Not Obligation

Responsibility is never an obligation. When responsibility is an obligation, it is really blame, shame, and guilt. That is a clever evasion of responsibility. Responsibility is the direct realization of cause. You caused it. Now what?

Responsibility freely chosen is incredibly empowering. Why do you think Christ and Gandhi used it to directly change the world? It is the hallmark of divinity.

When you take responsibility as an opportunity, whether another endless war, climate change, or monetary crises, you look forward to transforming the situation through the power of Universal Consciousness, Universal Love, and Universal Presence.

Honor Your Word

It works best to keep your agreements. If you ignore them, or change them capriciously, you make your job and that of others needlessly convoluted. The more you honor your word, the more things flow. You begin to enjoy your work a whole lot more.

When your agreements conflict, acknowledge the situation. You always have the option to consciously renegotiate the agreement so that it works for everyone involved. It is more than just keeping the rules. It is creating a game that is a joy to all players.

You will realize that you never have to be a slave to your agreements. Most people will give you a break when a given agreement is shown as unworkable. Most people truly want you to win.

Divinization

Life is a process of becoming the divine being you ultimately are already. You are a son or daughter of the living God. You are a spiritual being playing human for a time. This means that your animal nature, as a human, need not have command over you.

The divine part of you can grow to have pre-eminence in all you think, feel, and do. Your body, your mind, your humanity are all precious gifts to play in this divine love story we call life.

A most important insight is that you never need PLAY God when you fully realize that you ARE God. Playing God is an expression of powerlessness. God doesn't need to prove Himself. Only mortals do. Remember who you are and what this is all about.

Love Everyone and Everything

When you take full responsibility, you can't help but love everyone and everything. We are all equally human and divine. Nothing really happens by accident. Other people are here to enrich your experience. No one really wants to do it all alone.

When you recognize that you, yourself, are a total rascal, you can laugh it off on the rest of us. You don't have to be straight, righteous, or totally together to receive love. You receive love simply because our Source loves you with an absolute love, much like an infinite, eternal bonfire.

Fathers and mothers love their sons and daughters even when they are being naughty. Being mischievous is a mark of growing up. How then can the Creator hate us when we are behaving like a fool? God IS love, and so are we.

Own Your World, Heal Your World

When you own your world, you can heal it with your very love. You naturally love what you create. You recreate in your day-to-day experience everyone and everything. The good and the bad, we are all your creation, and so are you to us.

Your very love is what heals your creation, whether in the hospital, the battlefield, or the nursery. The more comfortable you are sending love to everyone and everything you encounter, the more you become a spiritual master who never has need of justifying his or her life.

If you dwell on this, you will grasp the implications. As a son or daughter of the living God, you have no limits whatsoever to move, touch, and inspire the billions of us living around the planet. Not only that, but you also have the power within you to love everyone who ever lived, or whoever will live. You always have direct access to Absolute, Universal Love.

Remember

- Taking 100% responsibility for your experience means you "own" everyone in your field of awareness.

- Responsibility has nothing to do with blame, shame, or guilt, which are actually clever evasions of responsibility.

- When you own your experience, it has a healing effect on everyone who interacts with you.

CHAPTER FOUR

Beyond Theology:
From Good News to Glorious News

Most of us have been exposed to the Christian Gospel in some form or other. Along with it, we too often discover a distorted theology that misses the whole point and leaves us with an inescapable sense of guilt.

Historically, two critical points were sidelined by many people who shared the Good News.

First, Christ died not to shield us from an Angry God about to destroy us, but rather to reveal a Loving Father who cherishes and adores us.

Second, while Christ is the Son of God in a very special way, so are all of us in our own way. We are all inherently divine. When we look directly into His eyes, we will see not only God made visible, but our truest self, our highest possibility, made visible.

We therefore move beyond "Good News," which implies "Bad News," to truly "Glorious News."

Inherent Divinity

One of the leading blind spots in the Christian tradition was the failure to recognize that "made in the image of God" means that we all share a divine nature. In truth, a number of early church "Fathers" emphasized that salvation, or transformation, was universal; all-inclusive. The Gospel narrative was a vehicle to awaken us to our one and only True Self, which we call "God."

When we reflect on the implication of being sons and daughters, we realize that we must be infinitely precious in the eyes of our Creator. We inherit eternal life from our Father and enjoy full access to His power and glory.

Christianity, as it was meant to be, is all about transformation at the heart level. You could see the Buddha powerfully transforming the mind. Jesus took it to an even deeper level, transforming our very heart, the center of our being.

Never into Counting Points

Our Creator never was into counting points; we were. We might see the Ten Commandments as a curse; that Moses offered them to us as a way of trapping us. We fail to realize that it was a way of showing us how we could live in communion with our Creator. A religion of counting points is the way a child thinks, never appropriate for maturity.

Too often, we reflexively conceive of the Creator, based on the Old Testament, as a schizophrenic monarch in the sky throwing down thunderbolts. This is an idolatrous image based upon the Greek's royal god, Zeus, who was fond of scaring his subjects to keep them in line, much like the ancient monarchs.

Love, alone, is sufficient to fulfill any divine injunction. All the rules are fulfilled by a love that can flow spontaneously through you. And it is yours for the asking!

Ultimate Demonstration

The cross wasn't so much required to appease an angry God as to demonstrate for all time the love of our Divine Father. The atonement theology too often preached from the pulpits is that God can't stand us. He thus had to sacrifice His own son to make us at least tolerable. By contrast, the theology of Saint Francis is a creation theology. Christ died as the ultimate expression of a Love that never gives up on us.

You could see Christ standing in place of all humanity to show how nobody need despair of his or her worth. The implication is that you are infinitely precious to our Creator. If that seems strange, it is because you were conditioned by people with a very limited understanding of the Gospel message.

The cross was written into the story of humanity from the very beginning. It turns out that this is the greatest love story ever told. As the great English poet, John Milton, put it, "The Fall from the Garden of Eden was a *Fortunate Fall,* as it allowed God through Christ to conclusively demonstrate what His Love is all about."

Resurrection Triumphant

The Eastern Orthodox tradition focuses on the resurrection of Christ as the resurrection of each one of us. The resurrection transforms the icon of the cross into an expression of utter triumph against all odds, against all opposition. The Christian faith is all about certain victory, not endless defeat.

This inspired narrative shows how we no longer need fear death, as death, itself, has been made the gateway into eternal life. It is no accident that our generation, the generation that has seen the whole world come together, is the very one to awaken to a multitude of near-death experiences attesting to the overpowering Love that awaits us.

The LORD OF LOVE has *already* won the war. If this Love can overcome death, itself, what can it NOT overcome? Just because so very few Christians have thought out the full implications of their faith does not make this proclamation false.

From Eternity Past to Eternity Future

When Jesus proclaimed, "Your sins are forgiven," it was not for that moment only, but forever. All your past failures have been blotted out in the eyes of the ONLY ONE who truly counts, the LORD OF LOVE. This is a divine love story. Were it any different, we might have cause for dismay.

Your present inadequacies can be replaced by access to infinite power. All you need do is to awaken to this power. We suffer because we believe in a limited God whose love is strictly conditional on our performance.

Your future destiny is never in doubt, as it is no longer up to you, but the LORD OF LOVE, Himself. You need not preoccupy yourself with getting better but begin to express your inherent perfection. You are already whole, complete, and perfect in His eyes.

Reconciliation of the Whole World

In the Glorious News, Christ came not only for Jewish people, Christians, and Muslims, but for *all* humanity. The divine narrative abolished outcasts. Every human being who ever lived is our brother and sister. Jesus went out of His way to hang out with so-called "sinners." People who stumble often get it much faster than the rest of us.

The LORD OF LOVE is also the LORD OF THE UNIVERSE made visible, as love conquers all. When we think of the Beatles, the one song that will remain forever is "All You Need Is Love." As the most acclaimed rock group in history, the Beatles had wide open access to all the pleasures of life. It is noteworthy that they ended up with total clarity on what matters most.

The world only needs to awaken to an accomplished fact. It is no longer about this person or that person's religion. It is the full realization that God IS Love.

Redemption of Planet Earth

In the Glorious News, planet Earth with all its plants and animals will be transformed into paradise. Environmentalists will be so relieved to know that this narrative is inclusive of all of life, not just people. Creation is exquisitely beautiful. Redemption means to restore it all to pristine innocence and beauty, much like awakening from a nightmare and finding your postal code in paradise.

Contemporary science is revealing that everything we experience can be expressed as information. All that is needed is to recall the information we thought we lost. That is why the Gospel is not so much good news, with bad news attending it. It is about truly glorious news. Win | Win | Win. Winning all the way around.

The lion and the lamb will characterize the ultimate world order. This need not be taken literally. The great romantic poet, William Blake, marveled that He who made the lion also made the lamb. When you realize that you now live in a divine love story, you will find your life so much easier.

Everything That Ever Happened, HAD to Happen

Our great story is a perfectly crafted divine love story with no accidents. However, when we are right in the middle of the action, things can seem random and chaotic. Our task is to keep bringing ourselves back to the Truth: *Absolute Unity, Absolute Love, Absolute Perfection.* This is possible when we accept that there is ONLY God, and the Universe is but a living expression of that God.

When you go see a love story with a happy ending, who could the stars be but the lovers, themselves? Our opportunity is to become, like Christ, the greatest lover in *our* world. For such a love, the journey, itself, is the reward.

Think about the Oscar for Best Picture, such as that for *Shakespeare in Love.* We only appreciate what an exquisite work of art it is when we arrive at the very end. We find the story so wonderful that we want to play it over and over again.

"A World That Works for Everyone, with No One and Nothing Left Out"

Years ago, Werner Erhard and Bucky Fuller established the standard of win/ win relationships. A world that works for some, but not everyone, is not enough. A world that works for most people, but not you, is not adequate. Only Universal Love is up to the myriad challenges humanity now faces.

The great American President, John F. Kennedy, used to sail by a motto he put on the bell of his recreational boat, "Where we go one, we go all."

This type of cohesion is invincible. This spirit made America great, and it will make America great yet again.

When we commit wholeheartedly to win-win games, where everyone may play, and there are no losers, we will find that we live by the Golden Rule and play out our divinity on the game board of life.

Remember

- The cross of Christ was never about you being a filthy worm. It is all about God being madly in love with you, willing to do anything to awaken you to His Love.

- Christ didn't elect to die for you because you were hopelessly human, but because you were ineradicably divine.

- Christianity didn't begin with a broken cross, but with an empty grave. Resurrection is what it is all about!

CHAPTER FIVE

Sermon on the Mount: God Is Love

When we carefully study the world's greatest sermon by the Master Himself, we discover another dimension of Being where God is All in All, and the one rule is the Way of Love.

Christ dared to see all humanity as inherently divine. In pronouncing a kingdom, or world order, where Love reigned supreme, He revealed Himself, for all time, to be the Lord of Love. The more you come to know Him, the more appropriate this title will seem.

Love is not a form of weakness, but the expression of ultimate creative power. The entire Universe was created in an outpouring, or divine celebration, of Love. The Lord of Love is the Lord of the Universe. His kingdom is that of the heart.

You Are Here to Make a Difference

You will never truly be fulfilled until you contribute to a mission larger than yourself. As it is often said, "You can never get enough of what you don't really want."

When all your basic survival needs are met, other needs take precedence. You now are in a better position to impact more people's lives than at any time in history.

Rabbi Hillel in ancient Palestine asked, "If not now, when? If not us, whom?"

When you are truly responsible, you willingly seize the opportunity. When you get that few human beings who ever lived have had the opportunities we now have to impact our generation, and generations to come, you can rejoice at your timely birth.

The vast cloud of great people who have preceded us reveals that we have infinitely more potential than we dare realize. We need only think of Buddha, Socrates, Christ, Mohammed, Saint Francis, and Gandhi. They have all suggested that we could match or surpass their accomplishments if we could continuously tap into their divine consciousness.

Hold Yourself to a Higher Standard

Why try to be merely "good" when you can be truly great? The more focused you are, the more you can strive to attain excellence in your calling or pursuit. To be world-class in a skillset requires at least 10,000 hours of practice. We can definitely reach that level of proficiency in anything if we keep at it long enough. You will eventually find that you are only competing with yourself.

When you tune in to your passion, you begin to pursue excellence. When you are tuned in to your passion, you lose all sense of time. For example, I used to improvise on the piano for hours. It was as if there was no beginning and no ending. I then channeled this energy into initiating relationships, gaining the privilege of meeting thousands upon thousands of people.

Inner direction is the key to an extraordinary life. Our rational mind can take us only so far. Living by the norms of our society may keep us sane, but hardly inspired. When we look into the deepest part of ourselves, we encounter a power that can overcome any obstacle.

Always Rely on Inner Direction

No written code can bring out your magnificence as much as moment-by-moment divine guidance. As children, we often want rules to discover how best to get along. We are too young to appreciate all the nuances of life and we lack the rational discrimination we later will develop.

A formulaic life cannot compare with an inspired life. When we spiritually awaken, we find ways to go into the flow, where we attract what we desire spontaneously. At some point, we can go beyond the rules, much like a great artist. Einstein revealed through his incomparable thought experiments that imagination transcends intellect. In his *Annus Mirabilis* or "Year of Miracles" (1905), he wrote four papers that forever changed the course of physics.

We have become so accustomed to justifying everything we do that we automatically ask, "Why?"

We can easily turn that around to, "*Why not?*"

Often, there is no good reason NOT to do something. You are now free to create your own life.

Keep Things Simple with God

Consider God your best friend and talk to Him that way. Those of us who have had a conversion experience, or an experience of enlightenment where we meet our True Self, can imagine God as our best friend rather than our fiercest task master. As our buddy, God knows it all, everything we feel, think, say, and do. We can thus speak to Him much as if we were a four-year-old child.

As you relax into God through the years, God will open up to you. Moments of prayer will come spontaneously without your having to hang up the line with "Amen." You can always keep the line open.

The more you share with God, the more He will show you what is possible, more than you have ever imagined. When I was a child, I never supposed that I would be given the vision to bring every faith together in Love. I just realized as a Protestant that those who told me "All Catholics are going to hell" were deeply deluded.

Our Job is Never to Judge, but Always to Love

When you truly love anyone, you eliminate the need for judgment. It stands to reason that, when you judge another person, you will end up being held to the same standard. Why ever put yourself in that position? We are all human, including ourselves.

Most people gratuitously offer others way more judgment and evaluation than is needed. It takes years to realize that we were never set up to definitively judge or evaluate another. We are here to see the divine presence in every single person we encounter.

Whenever you offer others deep acceptance and heartfelt appreciation, they will invariably respond in kind. In our world, we rarely, if ever, get too much of that. What a wonderful feeling it is to give up forever the role of judge! If you do find yourself in that role, the way out it is to show compassion wherever possible.

Whenever God Comes First, Your Every Need is Met

When you continue to focus on God, you will operate on a much higher frequency. As you raise your vibration, you will begin spontaneously attracting what you need. You will experience enough abundance to start freely sharing what you receive.

The way the Universe is set up, you can't truly give to others without receiving more in return. Experts in prosperity consciousness assure us it will easily be ten times more, although not always directly from our recipients.

The fastest way to experience a cornucopia of prosperity is to start sharing whatever you have with others. As you put God first, realizing that God IS LOVE, this will become easier and easier.

Whatever You Want from Others, First Give to Them

Give to others the love they crave and watch them enthusiastically reciprocate. You may be beautiful, intelligent, affluent, and talented. All of that and more will not equal your ability to make those in your life feel wonderful. Make everyone you meet feel good.

We all want recognition, respect, and acceptance, and are eager to return that to whoever freely offers it. What does it cost you to recognize, respect, and accept the next person you meet? Only a wee bit of your time.

Since money is ultimately a sign of appreciation, appreciate everyone you pay, even if it is the tax collector! Very few of us are flooded with appreciation. Even the greatest movie stars crave it from time to time.

Love and Forgive Everyone

Everyone you meet is your mirror; love them, and you automatically love yourself. There are no accidents in life. Each person you encounter presents you with a whole new set of possibilities. When others are short on love, you can be sure that you are lacking, as well. You will eventually find that you can forgive God (as if God needed forgiveness), then your worst enemy, and finally, even yourself!

Make it a habit of systematically forgiving *everyone* you meet, if even for a day. When you do this often enough, you will realize you are never really all alone. Every friend was once a stranger, and every stranger will soon be a friend.

As you embrace the people in your life, however they may appear, you will begin to own your world. You will realize that you co-create with our Source moment by moment. Everyone and everything is a gift. Only God has the last word.

Welcome Your Worst Enemy

Your worst enemy is not there by accident; he is there to keep you on your toes. We only have enemies based on our own fears. When we cannot own our perceptions of someone else, we project the worst side of ourselves onto them. In fact, you can learn the most not from your friends, but from your opponents.

Your worst enemy is the most in need of your divine love. You don't even have to guess. When you confront your own dark side, you will have the space to see the divine in everyone, unconditionally.

The further you go in life, the more you will realize that your worst enemy is a great candidate to become your best friend. Fear and hatred are expressions of energy. When fear and hatred are transformed into love and trust, you will find extraordinary love for the very person you thought would do you in. This is wonderfully portrayed in the

Hollywood classic, *An Officer and a Gentleman*. Richard Gere, as Zack Mayo, realizes that his drill sergeant, Lou Gossett, Jr., as Sgt. Foley, actually made him into a real man and gave him the wings to fly.

Let People See God Through You

When you view everyone as a precious creation, they will see the Creator in you. Since God IS Love, and Love is your true nature, you, like St. Francis, can become an instrument of peace. People in India for centuries have greeted each other with "Namaste!"

This means that I salute God within you. Ultimately, this becomes God honoring God.

Our supreme injunction is to continuously demonstrate God, not only through our words, but through every thought and action. By allowing the divine to flow through us, it is possible for those we meet to find God, possibly for the very first time.

As God becomes increasingly present to you, He becomes more and more available to everyone in your path. When people begin to see God within you, you can dispense forever with trying to impress them. They will start loving you just the way you are.

Remember

- Who you are is utterly magnificent. We are incredibly blessed to have the divine incarnation declare our ultimate potential.

- Forgiveness is THE way to move forward in life. We are all awakening at the rate we are awakening.

- Neale Donald Walsch puts it, "Your life is not so much about you, but about everyone with whom you interact." You are an ambassador of the Kingdom of Love.

PART 2

Universal LOVE

Unleash the Most Powerful Force in All the Universe

The power within you is far greater than that which is in the world. When you find yourself in impossible circumstances, such as a global pandemic, a war, a forest fire, a hospital bed, or a depression, you only need to look within and remember the Lord of LIGHT, the Lord of LIFE, the Lord OF LOVE.

You are ineradicably divine. Our God is totally in love with you, as if you were the only ONE. In the Great Story, He both died for you and lives for you. He is training you to become a Master of LOVE; the Greatest Lover in YOUR WORLD.

Just as the sun shines every morning in clear skies or a blanket of clouds, you are commissioned to love everyone in our world with this same LOVE. This LOVE IS Salvation. This LOVE IS Eternal Life. If you are alive enough to read this, YOUR work, OUR work lies ahead. We already have everything and everyone we need to fulfill our destiny.

CHAPTER SIX

The Lord of Love:
Christ's Kingdom Finally Revealed

When people discuss the greatest human being who ever lived, the name of Jesus Christ usually comes to the top, or very near the top. Over two billion people around the world give Him at least nominal allegiance. You will even hear agnostics and atheists unwittingly swear by Him.

Many wars have been fought over the theological implications of Christ. So many people have been conditioned to view Him religiously, underplaying the immense contribution Christ has made to spirituality and mysticism.

When we see Christ as THE Lord of Love, so many of these issues resolve themselves. When you realize that Divine Love is the most powerful force in all the Universe, and Christ is the ultimate embodiment of that Love, you can only have unqualified adoration and reverence for Him. Who can argue with total transformation of the heart, from animal to human to divine?

Love is the Creative Force Behind the Universe

Our life began with an act of love. This fact is not so much promiscuous as enlightening. That which we take the greatest pleasure in is the root of our physical being on this planet. Should it be such a mystery that so much of our lives is preoccupied with sexuality?

In like manner, the Universe began in seconds with a Big Bang, emerging from nothing. As within, so without. It all began with vibration, or divine thought. "Let there be light, and there was light."

Every one of us resides in the Mind of God; the Heart of God.

Love validates life. Without Love, nothing really matters. Everything begins with Love. Everything is sustained by Love. Everything is utterly transformed by Love.

Relationship is the Very Heart of Reality

Fritjof Capra, with his brother Bernt's classic film, *Mindwalk*, revealed how relationship characterizes both reality and life. Capra created a revolution in contemporary physics by bringing East and West together in a bold reinterpretation of physics. Within atoms and subatomic particles, such as quarks, we can only define what we see by relationship itself. *This* is related to *that*.

Likewise, in *Mindwalk*, every tree grows in a dynamic relationship with every other tree, much like a symphony. Life is self-organizing. Everything grows together. A single note makes no sense. A single tree is a contradiction in terms. *Trees grow each other.*

The contemporary Franciscan Father, Richard Rohr, offers us all a daring grasp of the most abstruse of Christian doctrines, the Trinity, that God is three Persons in one. Father Richard suggests that we see God in us as sacred relationship, and that we are part of that very relationship, such that three becomes four, and the four becomes infinity. We are invited to join the circle of being in an endless dance.

God IS Love | Love IS God

If we accept that God IS Love, then we can accept that Love IS God. The New Testament provides the greatest revelation in three words: God IS Love. We imagine God as Spirit. Traditionally, we thought of God more in terms of the head than the heart. We had it all backward; we must first get it in the heart, then get it in the head.

Lust is biological; Love is spiritual. When we attempt to fulfill lust at the expense of love, we spiritually starve ourselves. Lust AND love go together.

Love is the fastest way to God. You can attempt to put an end to all thoughts and neutralize the drunken monkey of the mind. That might put you at the gate of the temple. Only love will take you to the very heart, the Sanctum Santorum of the temple. Love alone answers the *why* of life. Only love.

Our Lord is Madly in Love with Us!

The Gospel narrative reveals that Christ looks at us as His "Bride." Christ is God made visible. Divine humanity is the necessary counterpart. In the eyes of the Lord of Love, no one and nothing can take our place. Christ is the God-infused lover of all humanity. Only that Love which IS God can bring us all back together again.

The supreme sacrifice was willingly given to demonstrate a love that will never die. As Adam sided with Eve against God, so Jesus sided with us, refusing to enter Paradise without us. This love is rash; it won't think twice about giving up everything for the beloved.

When we accept the Spirit of Love, we are totally transformed. We fully realize that we were made for God, and God for each of us. Everyone eventually will respond to this Love because this Love is the very reason for his or her being.

Christ Arose in Utter Triumph

The Gospel narrative has Christ dying in surrender and being raised up as Lord of Lords. Our story can now start with victory, as the battle has ALREADY been won. While the central symbol of Christianity is the cross, it could easily have been the empty tomb. Love defies death.

When we come from our magnificence, we invite the possibility of a charmed life. When we realize that each of us is infinitely precious in the eyes of our Creator, we have license to live outrageously. We can focus on what truly matters rather than being totally caught up in the day-to-day exigencies of life.

As the early Christian hymns declared, "We are more than conquerors" through the power of Love. This love has more punch than a nuclear arsenal. Weapons can only destroy that which is visible. That which is invisible can heal everyone and everything. When we learn to channel this love, nothing will be too difficult for us to accomplish.

No One and Nothing Can Defy This Love

The Love behind the Resurrection can overcome anyone and anything. No one wants to fight against this kind of Love. A careful analysis of the Gospel accounts shows that Jesus Christ, fatally wounded and tormented, by all appearances was hopelessly dead. Yet defying all circumstances, Love restored Christ to a new life, far surpassing in glory anything that the Apostles could have imagined.

Love is the one thing of which no one can get too much. There is always room for more love. When it is overflowing, then it is freely given away for the asking to anyone and everyone. While infinitely precious, love has no price. Like rainwater, it lubricates the highways and erodes all opposition. All we need know is the Source of that love.

Love, itself, inspires and invokes Love in others. It is more viral than the plague. While the plague radically kills, love radically heals. We were conceived in love and brought to life in love. We are sustained by love. It is always a matter of paying it forward with this love. As it was given to us, so we share it with others.

Love Can Heal

Divine Love is the secret of the greatest healers. Jesus Christ was moved by compassion to work day and night. His very presence healed. Christ projected a divine energy that could literally touch people. He rapidly emerged as a superstar in His country of origin by providing immediate results. The people he touched made it totally clear that this all came from God. No one could conjure this up on their own.

Mary Baker Eddy's lofty principles of Christian Science were powered by Love. She wrote her classic guide to the Bible, *Science and Health with Key to the Scriptures*, with the proviso that the only magic formula required was love itself. Mary actually resuscitated people from the dead, along with healing every organ of the body, even broken bones.

Neem Karoli Baba, or Maharaji, the immortal guru of Ram Dass, had uncanny psychic abilities and could effortlessly read his followers' hearts and minds. Whatever he predicted came to pass. Maharaji could be seen at two places at once. He could burn rupee notes in a campfire and then pull them back out unsinged. After Maharaji transitioned, his closest students realized this was all done through Love; that his very Love was the true miracle.

Love Can Raise the Dead

Shakespeare's *Romeo and Juliet* vividly depicts the resurrecting power of love. In the story, Juliet, who eloped with Romeo against her family's wishes, had to fake her own death when Romeo was banished from the city. She would do whatever it took to join Romeo. The appearance of death would be just that, appearance.

Juliet went to the friar priest to procure a potion that could mimic death. After taking the potion, Juliet was then placed in the family tomb. The friar's hope was that she would awaken into the arms of her Romeo.

When Romeo failed to get the message that Juliet had only faked her death, in despair, he bought a fatal potion and drank it in the crypt next to Juliet's grave. When Juliet awakened to find her husband-lover fatally poisoned, she tried to drink his drained potion to no avail, then grabbed a knife and stabbed herself to death.

The underlying message of this incomparable romance is that Love Conquers Death, for after this tragedy, the "star-crossed lovers" of Verona heal their entire community of insurrection and civil war.

Love is Life Eternal

Love is stronger than death. Whenever you channel divine love to anyone, you discover eternal life in that very Love. Eternal life is eternal love. The one you love may transition, and you no longer see his or her face, but they are still very much with you. The Love, itself, is transcendent. That Love IS God.

As we begin to realize that we live in Divine Love, everything finally makes sense. We live in a divine love story starring the Lord of Love. We are all the beloved of the Supreme Lover; God made visible. Like Romeo and Juliet in Shakespeare's immortal play, nothing can ever separate us from that Love. There is only God, and God is playing each one of us as us. We are infinitely more than puppets; we are His precious children. When He remembers us, He awakens us, much like the buried Egyptian Pharaoh awaited immortality.

Whoever shares in that Love discovers their only True and Ultimate Self. Contemporary physics makes it very clear that we channel our thoughts and emotions from a source beyond our cells and molecules, from what the Hindus call the *Akashic Records*. Our brains are extremely sophisticated instruments that filter Infinite Intelligence so that God has a place to show up in the story.

Remember

- As we always exist in relationship, we find Love to be the creative force of the Universe.

- Since God IS Love, Love IS God. No one and nothing can possibly defy this power.

- Love unites, heals, and raises the dead. Love IS Eternal Life.

CHAPTER SEVEN

Forgiveness Forever:
An Accomplished Fact

Most of us have grown up with a conditional view of forgiveness, that you forgive someone *only if* he or she profusely apologizes and it is convenient for you to make up. You are reminded that forgiveness is not so much about your adversary as it is about you. If you hate your adversary, it does you no good. Just forgive him and move on.

We need a much larger understanding of forgiveness. There is no way to find God faster than to forgive and seek your own forgiveness. If your adversary is a mirror of your own shadow, and what you see in him also is visible in you, you make up for both your sakes. His well-being is as important as your own.

From the standpoint of the cross, history's greatest demonstration of Divine Love, we live in a context of absolute pardon and total forgiveness. Everyone, everywhere, for all time is equally forgiven. God IS Love. When we wake up to our divine identity, so are we.

You are a Son or Daughter of the Living God

Recognition of your divine nature allows you to feel, think, and act divinely. Too often, we feel that we are just a bunch of wretched clowns. You know that you have thought, felt, and done things to hurt other people, either intentionally or unintentionally. We look at ourselves in the mirror every morning and think petty, even nasty, thoughts. We hide our narcissism with carefully manicured masks that our friends never really buy.

The truth is that our Sacred Self lies within the deepest part of us. Way beyond your shadow, no matter how much of a character you are convinced you are, lies a love that defies any limitations you have set upon yourself. On the surface, you are a scamp or rascal. Just underneath, you are a scoundrel. If you applied to join a conscious community, you would, like Woody Allen in his Academy Award-winning Best Picture, *Annie Hall*, vote against yourself. Yet drill down far enough, into the very marrow of your bones, and YOU ARE LOVE. God is within you. This applies to both good citizens and apparent villains.

The God we worship, unlike a useless stone statue, is alive and omnipotent. There is nothing too difficult for that God. And we find that God is not so much in the sun and stars as in our very hearts. How difficult is it, then, to probe for the source of Love within our innermost being?

You Are Once and Forever Forgiven of All Your Failures–Past, Present, and Future

The heart of the Gospel is the realization that ALL our sins ARE forever forgiven. The narrative of the crucifixion of Christ established that God would do ANYTHING to bring us back. This is embedded in our Judeo-Christian heritage, no matter how hard the cancel culture might want to permanently delete it. This is so difficult for most of us to accept that we have historically sidelined it.

We are fixated on God as some Bogey Man in the sky rather than as our Ultimate Lover. This is why many spiritual traditions conceive of God as a gorgeous lady. The Hindus worship Her as Parvati, Kali, and Durga. The Catholic Church has enshrined the Blessed Virgin Mary as the mother of God. New Agers are preoccupied with the spiritual marriage of Mary Magdalene with Jesus of Nazareth.

When you truly awaken, you will find that there is actually no one out there to condemn you. The most touching story in the Gospel of John has an adulterous woman literally thrown into the presence of Christ, having been caught in the very act. Christ gazes at her, and then asks the self-righteous crowd, "Whoever among you that is without sin, let him cast the first stone."

He then looks down at the dirt and starts writing out characters. The accusers slowly depart, starting with the oldest. When they have all departed, Jesus gazes again at the adulterer and asks, "Woman, where are your accusers?"

She responds, "Lord, I have none."

The master then enjoins her, "Go and sin no more."

The power of this Love is incalculable.

Our Father Sees Only the LORD OF LOVE Within You

In identifying with Christ, it is as if God sees only Him when He looks at you. Since we live in a divine love story, all we need to do, like Romeo, is remember our lover. Christian theology interprets the eternal sacrifice on the cross, along with baptism and holy communion, to mean that God, when He looks at you, only sees Christ. As Saint Paul wrote, "He who knew no sin, became sin for us, that we might become the righteousness of God in Him."

The miracle is that your truest Self IS the Lord of Love. When we look upon the Messiah, the Avatar, the Boddhisatva of compassion, we are looking at who we will ultimately become, and who we ultimately are in this Love. Being recognized as divine, a son or daughter of the living God, you are called to be a Christ, a Buddha, a Krishna to your world, even as David Jones, Nancy Lee, Maria Garcia, or Rama Raj.

As Christ is God made visible, so ultimately are you. This may not even remotely seem the case. You may have already written yourself off, never hearing the injunction, "Please be patient with me. God is not finished with me yet."

One thing is clear. You are still alive. God has not written you off, and He is not finished with you yet.

Everyone You Meet is Your Mirror

Everyone, including yourself, you find within your own experience. You actually reside within everyone you meet, just as they reside within you. You have so become identified with your body/mind that you have practically forgotten your spirit. You are convinced that there is a world out there, and in that world, you don't count for much. This gets you off the hook from ultimate responsibility. This is your world, and everyone you meet is another you.

Ultimately, there is only one of us. The Witness in you, and the Witness in me, is that same Witness. This is true of the eight billion human beings alive today, even of the animals and plants that surround us. When you realize that you are God, and so is everyone else, and you, as you imagine yourself to be, don't really exist, then you are free.

Each of us is a uniquely precious expression of WHO WE ALL ARE. Just as no two snowflakes are alike and infinitely recursive fractals comprise the landscape around us, exquisitely beautiful, as we find in the Mandelbrot set, so are each of us precious manifestations of our Ultimate Self.

We are All Inveterate Rascals . . . God Only Laughs

When we finally realize we are all naughty and mess up a lot, we can take ourselves lightly. You know children are scamps, and yet you still love them. Since the ancient holy books have no smileys, we are utterly convinced that God has no sense of humor. Does mother and father have no clue that their kid is being naughty? Does that in any way affect their love for him? Do not parents occasionally laugh at their children, remembering how naughty they, themselves, used to be?

God is not looking for ideal people; He is looking for *real* people. A sinner is a saint who hasn't yet awoken. If you look at the greatest saints, such as Saint Paul or Saint Francis, they were anything but naïve. Saint Paul as Saul of Tarsus vigorously persecuted the early church. He was its nemesis. However, his stunning vision of Christ on the way to Damascus transformed him into the world's greatest single missionary. Francis of

Assisi loved to live it up as a youth and was a bit reckless and careless of others. When Francis became a knight, he blew it and got captured in battle and imprisoned in a neighboring city. When Francis was brought back to Assisi in defeat and shame, he finally discovered the birds, the lepers and Saint Claire. He woke up to become "the Second Christ."

When our pretense is dropped, we will be utterly stunned at how beautiful we all can be. God is not sitting in a cloud with a telescope peeping down at you. He sees you as infinitely precious, the apple of His eye. He sees all of us as His children, made in His image, destined for His glory.

God Doesn't Keep Points . . . We Do

All those ancient commandments were but a means to an end to show us our need for God. We love keeping points as a game of one upmanship. That way, we don't have to stay responsible for it all. This is a child's perspective. As soon as your son or daughter is old enough, as a blooming adolescent, you explain the purpose of all the house rules. As Saint Paul put it, the Hebraic law was but our tutor to take us to Christ to join the new humanity.

When we realize the only way to win the point game is to stop playing, we come to a place of surrender. As the film *War Games* brilliantly depicted, no one can win a game of thermonuclear war, so why not play a nice game of chess? As you keep trying to be "good enough" to qualify, you convince yourself you don't have it, masking your inner perfection.

God wants us as we ARE, not as we are supposed to be. As Christ put it before leaving this world, *Love is the only commandment.* Love God, love your neighbor, love your enemy, love even yourself. Love everyone and everything. If we politically comprehended this at a deep enough level, we would realize the more regulations you enact, the more infractions you get. We need institutions that totally transform us through That Love.

In the Divine Economy, Forgiveness is the Currency

To go farther and faster, start forgiving as if there is no tomorrow. Heaven is not so much me getting my reward but rather rejoicing in YOU getting YOUR reward. Not only do you forgive your adversary, but you actively work so that he or she may truly prosper. What would happen if you treated everyone in your life as your own brother or sister, father or mother, son or daughter?

You only become comfortable with your reward when it becomes OUR reward. It is never the little you that does it all. It is always a team effort. Any reward you receive is but an acknowledgement of others. As Andrew Cohen, the evolutionary enlightenment visionary expressed it, this is the HIGHER WE.

All glory ultimately goes to our only True and Ultimate Self, the Lord of the Universe. Every beat of our heart, every breath we take is but His grace and love in action. We are not here on this Earth a moment too long or a moment to short. His will brought us into being and will bring us with Him into ultimate triumph.

When You Forgive Anyone, They ARE Forgiven

Since God is NOT into the condemnation game, whoever you forgive IS forgiven. As an awakening being, your forgiveness is total. Forgiveness is the only game in town from a divine perspective. Of what use are grudges? All our judgments and evaluations come and go. Only Love is forever. God never has been in the judgment game and rejoices when you finally wake up. You, like Jesus of Nazareth, have the divine authority to forgive anyone in your life. There are never any villains, only precious souls for whom Christ died.

No one who has ever lived is incapable of being forgiven. Every generation cherishes their devils, whether Napoleon, Hitler, or the latest Russian or Chinese autocrat. We are all human beings. We are all so vulnerable to love that it can break us down into sobs. Your sins, OUR sins, ARE FORGIVEN.

When you see yourself in the worst of us, you will find your best self in them, as well. Every morning, for a good number of years, I have prayed blessing for whatever problem nations and leaders occur to me, especially my own here in the United States of America. If all of us only committed to unconditional love and forgiveness, if we could be ever mindful of God as ABSOLUTE LOVE, there is nothing we could not do.

Namaste Means Salute the Divine in All You Meet

Honor everyone as if they are God; they are, indeed, a unique expression of our Source. Few people will argue with you when you treat them as God. What a waste of time that would be! Can you imagine what would happen to diplomacy? We would witness an incomprehensible love fest around the planet on a scale never before imagined.

As your realization deepens, you will find that you never have to prove that YOU are God. There is nothing BUT God. What else could it be? Your body/mind, or little self, is a precious piece on the game board that lets you play. The real you is the Supreme Self of the Universe; the eternal subject that creates everyone and everything.

When your love is great, all the world opens to you. All the world loves a lover. Whether Elvis Presley or Leonardo di Caprio, people will flock to your show. Until now, you may have never conceived that you, yourself, could become the greatest lover in YOUR WORLD. You are a saint in the making. Begin to tap into the power within you that can make an absolute difference.

Remember

- Christianity is ultimately a school for Divine Love. Practicing forgiveness puts you in the fast lane.

- Rules serve an educational purpose to give you a glimpse of what it might mean to live LOVE.

- Our God is in love with you and only wants you to be who you truly are underneath all the costumes.

CHAPTER EIGHT

Power of Blessing:
Channel It Around the World

Mata Amritanandamayi (simply known as "Amma") has devoted her life to hugging people with a divine blessing. She has hugged literally millions of people over many years. Out of curiosity, I went to see her when she was visiting the San Francisco Bay Area. Amma spoke little or no English. She just sang hymns of praise before her mystified visitors.

When Amma hugged me, she spoke in Malayalam, her native language of the Indian state of Kerala. She just said something to the effect of "My darling, my darling, my darling." It was towards midnight, and I felt an unmistakable energetic lift.

Later the following year, I was hospitalized for surgery. From the beginning of the operation, I felt a surge of irresistible Divine Love that lasted the entire week. In my mind, I remembered Amma's blessing. *So this is it!*

Blessing is an Irresistible Force

Who would possibly object to your blessing them? When you bless people, you are honoring and upholding them and championing them to be the best possible version of themselves in this incarnation. *Blessing others makes you a master of life.* You can gradually remove all enemies from your life by refusing to consider them as "enemies."

Blessing others inspires them to bless you. As everyone is capable of giving blessings as well as curses, people would much rather give and receive blessings. When you believe in others, they begin to believe in you. We all want to prosper in every sense of the word. Blessing incalculably contributes to prosperity since it comes from a place of deep prosperity.

As you are blessed, you continue the virtuous spiral upward. There is no limit to blessing, as the entire Universe is bent in that direction. Whereas, *cursing is limited, as it destroys the very one who curses.* As the classical Greeks put it, "The gods make mad those whom they would destroy."

Blessing Leads to Profound Forgiveness

You will find to your amazement that *you cannot hate anyone you continue blessing.* As an experiment, try blessing the person at the top of your blacklist for the next thirty days. It could be someone you know personally, a prominent politician, or the head of another country. Just ask our Source, "Bless _____." You will find ill feelings will rapidly dissipate.

Blessing has a powerful, cumulative effect. I have blessed heads of state and problem countries around the world on a daily basis for over two decades. With the passing of every day, my feelings of love grow stronger. I spontaneously forgive them of whatever wrong I think they have done.

As you continue blessing those you hate, you, yourself, will be powerfully transformed. For example, I prayed for a particular Republican President from the day of his inauguration. Although HE didn't change, I changed profoundly. With certain Republican presidents, I have developed a deep fondness, as was the case with Ronald Reagan. I can now say the same of Donald Trump.

When You Bless Others, They ARE Blessed

When you bless people, the Lord of Heaven blesses them along with you. As a son or daughter of the Living God, you have the authority and the power to bless ANYONE, AND THEY WILL BE BLESSED. The power that lies within you is far greater than that which lies without.

In the Gospel narrative, God wants nothing more than that humanity come together in love. This is the new humanity, inherently divine. Blessing is the foundation. Christ opens up His supreme Sermon on the Mount with a repeated set of blessings.

As you bless others, you redeem their lives. *It takes only ONE person to truly believe in another.* It may be of interest that the Prophet Muhammed, blessed be his name, when he initially encountered the Angel Gabriel commanding him to recite, Muhammed, himself, feared that he had lost his mind. He sought clarity from his wife, who believed his story to be the truth. From that point, Islam grew to become a religion entailing nearly a quarter of the Earth's inhabitants.

Blessing Presences Divine Love

Bless others in the name of God, and they directly experience God. Everyone you encounter is a uniquely precious expression of our Creator. *They live and move and have their being only through God's blessing.* This is true even of people you consider impossible. They never tire of divine love.

Blessing is divine love made active. When you sincerely bless someone, it is like stopping them in their tracks. You move from theory to practice. The words of sacred scriptures jump out of paper and ink and become living, redemptive.

Blessing is THE fastest way to access divine love. A heartfelt blessing is telling God you get it in the most profound way. You can't lose with blessing. If you face a civil war, bless BOTH sides. Today, *anyone* involved in a war loses. Love and forgiveness are the only way to prevent it, and the only way to stop it.

The Impact of Blessing is Cumulative

The more you bless people, the more you want to bless them. It becomes addictive in a positive way and goes viral. Since our current world can't get too many blessings, people soak it up as it they were emotionally starving. They will gradually find themselves bound to you for life. Simply keep it up unconditionally.

Day after day, your blessings will get better and better. Blessing is so simple! You stay mindful of people and things, upholding them with a radiant energy, which keeps on growing. It doesn't cost you anything but a little time and energy. Yet it can give you almost anything!

Gradually, your own divine nature will become visible to you. While you no longer deny your shadow, you become totally focused on becoming the man or woman you were meant to be, a divine lover. Blessing is the pivotal point that can transform the whole world, since the world is ultimately inside YOU.

Blessing Awakens Us to Our One and Only True Self

As we continue blessing others, we finally become that which we truly are. We were meant to bless and be blessed. This is what it means to be divine, to have the Consciousness of Christ streaming through you as a chosen vessel. You are truly magnificent when you open up!

We start the circle of love by unconditionally blessing everyone we meet. Whatever race, nationality, gender, or religion, it doesn't matter. We are all children of the same God with infinite potential. As people are continuously exposed to unconditional Love, they blossom further than they ever imagined.

Eventually, we will only bless, and cursing will not even cross our minds. When you begin to see God in everyone and everything, you will have reason to rejoice. As the great spiritual traditions have taught us, there is no one and nothing beyond redemption. *Love is infinitely creative. Nothing is lost forever.*

Nothing is as it Appears to Be

The more people seem unworthy of your blessing, the more they need that blessing. We are never in a good position to judge others. It just takes some of us a whole lot longer to fully "get it." No matter how despotic or how beaten down we may be, God dwells within the nucleus of our being. We will totally respond to that Love which IS God.

A Christian psychologist, Dr. Clyde Narramore, once maintained, "Every person is worth understanding."

Dr. Carl Jung, the father of depth psychology, saw all of us as fragmented. For Dr. Jung, therapy was a process of bringing together all the broken pieces, throwing light on the shadow. What shines out from there is the treasure of all treasures, The Self.

When the secrets of their story are unraveled, you will find that you are looking at an angel. How many of us had happy childhoods? How many of us had all the breaks? How many of us didn't mess up in major ways early in our lives? The greatest "sinners" make the greatest saints because they have learned the hard way to deeply appreciate the Light.

Bless Both Individuals and Nations

You can start today by blessing entire countries and their leaders. Blessing transcends time and space. In 2022, Russia went to war against the Ukraine, unilaterally invading it. On the surface, this looks unpardonable. However, *there are always deeper reasons*. For several hundred years, the Ukraine was considered an integral part of the Russian Empire. This doesn't justify anything. It just means that both countries need our prayers.

Nations act much like individual people. As harmony can be created between any two individuals, so harmony can be created between any two nations. It might be at great cost. However, it is possible. Always, people are involved. Invisible forces prompt people to do what they do; however irrational their behavior may appear.

Rulers need blessing even more than their people. They assume huge responsibility. Most people lack their courage and commitment. Condemnation never does any good. *Gratitude, blessing,* and *forgiveness* become invincible. The Christian faith grew out of the Roman empire under periods of immense persecution. As the saying goes, "The Church was sewn by the blood of the martyrs."

Within several centuries, Caesar, himself, became a Christian.

Your Destiny is to Become the Very Avatar You Worship

Whoever you worship, you will finally become. Emulate God incarnate, and you gradually become Christ. This is the whole point of the Christian faith. The very word, "Christian," literally means "Christ in you." Jesus of Nazareth, as a divine rabbi, literally trained not simply His apostles, but the entire world. His principles and consciousness can never be stopped.

When you look at Christ, you are gazing into the mirror at your ultimate Self. Throughout His Earthly ministry, when channeling the greatest miracles, Christ continuously maintained that everything they saw was done by the Father, our Supreme Source. Furthermore, they would channel even greater miracles than Christ. This is actually borne out with a careful study of the New Testament.

We fool ourselves by supposing that Christ only died for the person next to us, but never directly for us. This gets us off the hook of being totally responsible. To fully realize that ANYONE would love us to THAT extent leads to only one thing, *total surrender in love, to be an agent of transformation the world over.*

Remember

- When you bless everyone and everything, that blessing transforms your experience of the world.

- As you keep blessing people, the impact often becomes exponentially more powerful.

- Try blessing on a consistent basis those at the top of your blacklist and see what happens.

CHAPTER NINE

Prayer: How to Start a Conversation with God

It may seem strange to talk to someone entirely invisible. However, since smart phones, people don't hesitate to talk to specific people nowhere to be seen, all while cords dangle from their ears.

Many people think of prayer as a one-way conversation where you hope God, like Santa Claus in the North Pole, will pull the right item from the Amazon catalog and swiftly dispatch it to you. They never think God will take the trouble to call them back.

The word "prayer" originally meant request. God is the ultimate concierge. He obliges us because He wants a relationship with His creation. But true prayer goes way beyond this to include discussing *anything* with God.

Invite God to Reveal Himself / Herself to You

You can come to God with all your doubts and ask Him to show up for you. You don't even have to believe in any God. Try this as an experiment: If you once believed in God, but lost your faith, invite him to demonstrate His reality to you once and for all.

Be open to the Truth wherever it may lead, whatever the response. This will be an opportunity to discover the Transcendent Mystery and Supreme Identity to which we commonly refer as God. It is vital that you discover God for yourself, beyond mere belief, to establish your own relationship with Him.

Utterly sincere people usually discover their own truth about God. It goes way beyond any dictionary definition. You can study every single religious tradition only to realize you, yourself, must arrive at an authentic relationship to, and direct experience with, our Source.

Invite God to Occupy You

Whenever you sense God's presence, ask Him to come on in. When you call on a sacred name of God, as if He were in the neighboring room, you may be shocked by how fast He responds. Imagine God as the perfect human being, just as we think of Jesus Christ. Ask Him to enter your heart and soul.

Ask God a Question

To initiate a two-way conversation, ask God any question that occurs to you. Ask about the truth of any condition or situation. If you happen to feel sick, ask Him if you really ARE sick. You may be surprised to find that the answer is, "No, you are fine just the way you are."

Ask God what will happen in the near-term. You might be concerned about a shortage of cash, a conflict at home, a forest fire in the vicinity, or a new war erupting on the other side of the world. If it is not a frivolous question designed only for curiosity, you will very often find a rapid response.

Ask about how you can best fulfill your destiny. What would be His will for your life? Open your eyes and ears. Hang out with the query. Very often, impressions, if not subvocal words, will emerge. Often strange situations will emerge that later can be seen as the answer.

Listen for His/Her Voice

Whenever you ask God a question, stop and listen very carefully. On rare occasions, God may speak to you audibly. Neale Donald Walsch, who wrote the best-selling book series *Conversations with God*, got very upset with life one night. Neale was shocked to hear spoken words answering his challenge. Neale went on to grab a yellow notepad and record the conversation. Later, the Voice came to him internally.

Rather than condemn you, God's voice will supersaturate you with the utmost love. You might expect thunder and lightning, or a huge spanking from Grandpa up in the sky. The voice is more like a mother who truly loves you, or even a lover who adores you!

Many times, God will speak to you in the flow of your actual life experience. Neale claims that God is speaking to all of us all the time; we just don't listen. You need a change of heart and mind. You need to tune in. Suppose that nothing that occurs to you is purely by accident. You may end up observing spectacular coincidences. For example, you may run into the same person over and over in the same day, each time totally unexpectedly.

Identify the True Voice of God

Should you hear many voices within you, know that God's voice is always pure love. Should inner voices condemn you, know that they are most definitely not from God. The Bible calls those kinds of voices "Satan." Satan means "slanderer." You can never do anything right. You are bound for hell. All these kinds of things.

When you have uncertainty around a response you think you have received, ask the question three times. You will soon find it is always the Voice of Love that you can count on. If that Voice is not what you are hearing, keep asking. Eventually, you will intuitively respond to the divine voice. As Jesus Christ put it in the Gospel of John, "My sheep hear my voice." (John 10:27) Christ's voice has a signature key, a certain vibration in the cosmos that you will instantly recognize. I say this not simply from doctrine, but from my own actual experience.

God is ALWAYS on your side, consistently wanting only the very best for you. Not all of us had happy childhoods or flawless parents. Many times, the father can be harsh and demanding with his first child because he is inexperienced as a parent and working much harder and longer than he would like. God is different. He is Father, Mother, Son,

Daughter, Brother, Sister, even Lover. This is a total paradox. But without this paradox, God wouldn't be "God."

Spontaneous Prayer

Talk to God anytime you feel like it, much as a young child talks to Mom and Dad. You never need impress God with fancy words. As Christ puts it, He already knows what you want before you ask. What is challenging to realize is that God adores you, even when you have been naughty or messed up in a major way.

God delights in our simple trust and reliance upon Him, moment by moment. Prayer is a practice for US that totally works. It would seem that a God of Love totally yearns for our fellowship and is never too busy to take our call.

God answers you back in extreme situations within seconds. A few years back, I was stopped by a police car in a foggy area. The officer stopped me for using my high beams, but then said he was about to arrest me because I had a major problem with my license. I silently asked, "Oh God, please get me out of this!"

Suddenly, he changed his mind and said my partner could drive, and that I needed to fix things up with the Department of Motor Vehicles (DMV).

Petitionary Prayer

Ask God without any hesitation for what you truly need. No request is too big or too small. It seems that God is pleased when you ask Him for everything. His resources are infinite. Since He is actually in love with us, this is his greatest joy. As an ancient prophet asked, "Is anything too hard for God?" (Genesis 18:14)

Whenever there is a delay, maybe you asked for a brand new Tesla Model S, something even better is in store for you. Very often, we ask for things when we are not ready. Often, immediately manifesting something would be against our long-term interests. If you keep the faith, you will be glad you did.

Keep repeating important requests until they are answered. Strangely, Jesus gave a story to illustrate it. If you have an urgent need for something right in the middle of the night, you may decide to wake up your neighbor. Although she doesn't feel like obliging you, she will grudgingly get up on account of your very persistence.

Scientific/Metaphysical Prayer

Realize the truth of Who you are, regardless of any outward circumstances. You could meditate on the truth that you are whole, complete, and perfect just as you are. The essential you is divine. Often, should you feel sick, you will find that the feeling of illness will suddenly evaporate. This approach was perfected in Christian Science by the phenomenally gifted healer, Mary Baker Eddy.

Christ, when confronted with the greatest challenge of His earthly career, resurrecting a close friend who had been dead for four days, made a simple prayer: "I thank you for hearing me always." (John 11:41)

He then proceeded to do that which, by all reckoning, was clearly impossible. God hearing us always is a truth we can count on in challenging circumstances.

If you have severe self-esteem issues, for example, you feel you couldn't sell diapers to a pregnant woman, remind yourself that you are an infinitely precious child of the Living God. Too often we limit ourselves by ignoring fundamental truths surrounding our Divine Self.

Affirmative Prayer

Give thanks for the desired outcome well in advance of its manifestation. When you sense your request is in line with the will of God, you can have total confidence. For example, when you forgive your worst enemy, bless him, and affirm his highest good, you won't have the slightest doubt that God will respond. This is the highest priority in the Kingdom of God. It is literally bringing in the Kingdom to YOUR world.

Always allow the answer to manifest for the highest good of all concerned. For example, if you seek an extremely beautiful woman as your mate, she has free will. You may not be *her* highest good. However, if you ask for a beautiful woman LIKE this particular lady, you are opening the door to much deeper satisfaction.

Always allow the answer to be even better than what you imagined. Much of the time, we are out of touch with what we truly want. Silence from God may be part of the process of your arriving at what you TRULY want. As the saying goes, "We can never get enough of what we don't really want."

Structured Prayer

Combine prayer and meditation, repeating the same thoughts every day. You might start with praise, gratitude, and blessing. This will put you into a productive frequency. I have been reciting a prayer for people and nations. I am upholding them, regardless of circumstances. (See *Structured Prayer* in the Appendix.)

Reciting prayers of blessing has an overpowering cumulative effect. For example, when a president that I loathed took office, I would begin blessing him every day, whatever he said or did. I ended up loving him, regardless of my political persuasion. In addition, I prayed for North Korea for well over a decade before icy relations with the USA began to thaw.

This approach gives you the opportunity to bless *everyone* and *everything* in your life. You begin to realize that it doesn't matter how many reservations you have about the people and nations for which you pray. Your attitude will be transformed. You will find that you are in relationship. You will find a power emerge within you more powerful than any opposition.

Remember

- Prayer is a two-way conversation with God, who is always speaking to us through various channels.

- The True Voice of God is always love. Think of God more as your lover than your disciplinarian.

- There are many ways to pray. Nothing beats talking as a little girl to her mother or a little boy to his dad.

CHAPTER TEN

Meditation:
How to Let Go and Let God

Meditation is the art of listening to your innermost voice. It is the art of hearing the Transcendent speak through many different media, all the senses, your very breath. Much of the time, no one is listening. When you stop to listen, you may very well hear the voice of God.

You don't have to be religious. You just need an open heart and an open mind. You prepare quiet time where you close your eyes, breathe deeply, and watch your thoughts fly by. You will often hear God speak to you through your intuitive mind.

Just as you don't have to speak English to hear God's voice, you don't have to have spiritual training in either the East or the West. Like a shaman, you can learn to trust your Higher Self and commune with Pure Being.

New Age/Ambient Music
Soft music can place you into a trance, establishing a lush atmosphere whenever you close your eyes. New Age music, along with ambient music, was deliberately constructed to alter your consciousness. Much of it helps slow down your brain waves, heightening your creative imagination.

This music can be overwhelmingly positive, occasionally inducing states of ecstasy. Most often, it is purely instrumental, which makes it effective for contemplation. It can often be used to set the mood for deep meditation.

This music can bring in the most enchanting aspects of nature, such as a forest or seaside, without your needing to take a single step outside. Nature, itself, is often the environment where people most easily experience God. Think of how often poets borrow from the outdoors.

Transformational Art

Certain art seems to have a magical quality, especially when conveying deep beauty or even the miraculous. The Psychedelic Renaissance has inspired paintings that transport you into a fantastic alternate world. Renewed interest in psychedelics is exposing more and more people to altered states of consciousness in a relatively safe environment.

When you tour enough art galleries in a single day, you may find yourself "stoned." You develop what I call the *aesthetic response*, where the ordinary environment comes alive with beauty and ecstasy. With heightened sensibility, you will find that beauty is to be found everywhere.

Sacred art in Christian, Hindu, and Buddhist traditions can inspire the most exalted states. One need only think of Michelangelo's masterpiece, *the Pieta*, where the Blessed Virgin is holding the crucified body of her Son, Jesus Christ. Although the literal subject matter is both shocking and heart-rending, the depiction is rendered exquisitely beautiful through one of the greatest sculptors of all time.

Mystical Poetry

Most of the world's sacred scriptures are written in stunning poetry, often lost in translation. For example, the *Holy Qur'an* in Arabic is considered to be so beautiful that only God could have inspired the words. Unlike the Bible, which offers us endless stories, the *Qur'an* offers us the Voice of God directly addressing the human condition through the music of words.

The supreme Sufi master of the Middle Ages, Jalaludine Rumi, has amazingly become America's most popular poet through the genius of his contemporary translator, Coleman Barks, disciple of the profoundly mystical twentieth-century master, Bahaudeen. Coleman empowers Rumi with the voice of a twenty-first century lover who knows us intimately.

The Nobel Prize-winning Peruvian poet, Pablo Neruda, succeeded in making ordinary objects, plants, and animals glow with spirit. It was as if he were stoned out of his gourd. More likely, as he was a connoisseur of fine wine, it was intoxication by the fireplace. Pablo succeeded in making everyday experiences sacred.

Chanting

Whether Gregorian chant or praise to Lord Krishna, chanting can profoundly alter our consciousness. The repetition of certain words becomes truly hypnotic. Who hasn't listened to the Krishna people in a park endlessly chanting *"Hare Krishna, Krishna Hare! Hare Rama, Rama Hare?"* The words glorify the divine names until they supersaturate your consciousness.

When an entire group of people utter a chant, the effect becomes many times more powerful. You can get recordings where hundreds of people keep chanting together the sacred syllable, "om," which captures the pulse of the Universe.

To become God-conscious, keep repeating His sacred names over and over. Islam gives us 99 official names of God. Both Judaism and Christianity supply dozens of additional names. Taoism gives us the ultimate name, the Nameless. Perhaps the sound of the ocean, a gentle wind, or the gurgling of a bubbling stream.

Sacred Songs

Whenever we hear hymns or Christmas carols, we experience our most exalted moments. Sacred hymns have become indispensable to powerful evangelists. Billy Graham, one of the all-time greatest, had his partner, George Beverly Shea, sing the most powerful alter call ever written, "Just as I am."

These songs were meant to throw people into a transfixed state of being. They became vital to the expansion of Christianity around the world. If you sit down and read the words from a hymnal, they are powerful enough to bring you to tears. We are far more moved by our hearts than our heads.

All you need to do is surrender to these glorious melodies to be swept along. Virtually every great spiritual tradition will have its version of sacred hymns or sacred songs. Increasingly, you will hear modern and contemporary songs by pop musicians written over the last several decades.

Contemplation

Contemplating the true, the good, and the beautiful, we find ourselves becoming these qualities. You can contemplate the Messiah, an Avatar, or a Boddhisattva and gradually transform into them. Most often, you will recall stories that bring them to life. Gradually, you will see yourself becoming more like them. Christ is ultimately the perfection of Who you *already* are.

You can also simply keep contemplating the word "LOVE" and become it. This word has powerful associations that will trigger powerful, healing memories. By the Law of Attraction, the more you focus on Love, the more you will draw it to you. Your illusory self will slowly give way to your Divine Self.

Contemplation can very often lead to God Consciousness, where you begin to see only God in everyone and everything. For Christians, you see Christ in everyone and everything. In the process, you channel that very love, from which no one can separate you.

Mantra Meditation

Transcendental Meditation^{TM} has popularized the most essential method of all the Great Traditions. Mantras are initially given out loud and then repeated more and more softly until inaudible. Many years ago, I was given a mantra, which I still recall. It was drawn out of Hindu or Jyotish astrology, based upon my date, time, and place of birth.

When mantras are subvocalized, they serve to screen out your thoughts. Most of us in the West have a drunken monkey mind that chatters away whether we like it or not. It will frantically insist you listen to its rantings. The mantra serves as a point of concentration that will rapidly reduce your thoughts.

Eventually, the chattering will fade away, and you will get increasing gaps of pure consciousness. You will experience a kind of bliss. Even if it is just in flashes, the mantra will have a powerful impact. Your pattern of brainwaves will slow down to the point where you will experience deep relaxation, even accelerated sleep, where a few minutes or an hour or two will be sufficient to fully restore you to vibrant awakeness.

Silent Meditation

One of the most advanced methods is called *seedless* meditation or *meditating upon nothing*. When you have used a particular mantra long enough, you will feel comfortable trying it without the mantra. The mantra, itself, is simply skillful means to bring you completely into the present.

With an experienced meditator, the mantra will often go on by itself when not intentionally thought. The great *Maha siddhi* master of the Himalayan foothills, Neem Karoli Baba, kept writing the name "Rama," filling up an entire notebook. When the master sat in profound contemplation, he *became* the mantra, he *became* Lord Rama.

To hear and see what is there without thought brings about unmatched clarity, as is often found in Zen Buddhism. In Zen, you *just* sit, you *just* eat, you *just* listen. You add nothing to it. You allow that which is to be. As I learned from the *est* training years ago, when you put what is *there*, *there*, it just disappears, and pure space emerges.

Yogic Meditation

In the West, Hatha Yoga has developed into a practice beyond simply relaxing the body. Hatha works even when its practitioners are totally distracted. The posture exercises move your spine and limbs in many different positions. As you keep gently stretching for months and years, you become much more agile and poised.

At the end of a sequence of postures, it is quite natural to sit and meditate for a while. Eventually, you become aware of the various tensions, aches, and pains you feel throughout your body. They will subside, and you then experience your breathing, and your thoughts begin to slow down.

Going through the various postures, even without a formal relaxation period at the end, is a type of meditation. Vinyasa yoga encourages a continuous flow from one posture to another, almost like ballet. You experience a delicious lightness of being. Very often, you will walk away feeling totally energized.

Entheogens

Psychedelics like LSD, mescaline, and 5MeO-DMT can often catalyze a direct experience of God. The word "entheogen" implies putting God straight into you, just as the word "enthusiasm" implies being filled up with God. Each entheogen acts as a catalyst to remove the normal filters in our mind that mediate raw experience.

All natural psychedelics, such as marijuana, psilocybin, and mescaline, were originally used as part of sacred ceremonies. Carlos Castaneda's shamanic guru, Don Juan, called them powers or *allies*. They are skillful means to arrive at rare states otherwise extremely difficult to reach.

When led by an experienced guide to find God, these psychedelics may prove of great value. However, used carelessly, they can lead to psychosis, especially 5MeO-DMT. In doses over 10 mg of MeO-DMT, people have undergone Post-Traumatic Stress Syndrome (PTSS) with unpredictable flashbacks. In any event, bear in mind that both your mindset and the setting, itself, will impact the quality of your experience. Even the notorious drop-out professor, Dr. Timothy Leary, recommended caution whenever taking psychedelics.

Remember

- Meditation is simply a relaxed, receptive state of mind with slower brain frequencies.

- While you can practice meditating with a mantra, many other modalities may work just as well.

- Art, music, and poetry are staples for meditation, as are parks, forests, and seashores.

CHAPTER 11

Gratitude: Gateway to Abundance

Gratitude forms the basis for love that few people sufficiently appreciate. While we may routinely say, "Thank you," occasionally, we respond deeply from the heart. Everything we have comes from other people, and ultimately from our Source. By acknowledging this, we put ourselves in the way of prospering. Money, itself, is a direct form of appreciation.

As we appreciate other people, we give them something of which they never can get too much. When it comes from the heart, it rarely goes unnoticed. We can express our gratitude in myriad ways. Any way we do it, we can make a difference in other people's lives.

The more abundance you feel, the more readily you will express unconditional love for even those with whom you may be in competition. When you realize that there is room enough to appreciate everyone, you unleash the most powerful force in all the Universe, Divine Love.

Thank Your Way to Wealth

The more thankful you are of all you have, the more inviting you are to what you don't yet have. Count your blessings to remove any feeling of desperation or lack. Despite all appearances, our Universe is inherently abundant, no matter how hard human beings try to ruin it.

People want to give to those who appreciate their offering. The appreciation you give can be of much greater value than the gifts people bestow. Your very gratitude is a precious resource that can grow and glow. If you are thankful enough, there is nothing you cannot achieve.

Gratitude inspires positive thought forms, which gradually manifest into reality. With a foundation of gratitude, you are more apt to bless, forgive, create, enlighten, and empower. You will find that there is ALWAYS someone or something to be grateful for. It may be your very next breath!

Keep Running List of Thank Yous

Give thanks every day for anything or anyone that occurs to you. You can start by recalling all your breakthroughs. It may be as simple as tying your shoestrings, or as profound as winning a gold medal in the Olympics. It may be simply reaching out to a single person the moment they need your help.

Recall all the people who have enhanced your life in any way, whether a primary school teacher or a professional mentor that helped you establish your career. It may even be a difficult supervisor who caused you to stretch. At the time, you may have not relished it, but later you found his role was exactly what you needed at that particular time.

Recall all your sudden windfalls, whether an unexpected inheritance, a tax break, or a $100 lottery ticket. Initially, you may only identify a couple. As you continue this practice, you will notice hundreds throughout your life. Someone up there has been looking out for you!

Thank God for What You Already Have

When you begin to appreciate what is right in front of you, the more value you get from it. Think of all the items in your closet that you have all but forgotten. At one time, they were important to you, or you wouldn't have kept them this long. It could even be the mailman who helps you keep in touch with the world.

Thank God for all your friends and relationships. Everyone you know, even your family, was once a total stranger to you. Gradually, they came into your life. They each supplied you with warmth, love, and companionship, even if just a little bit. Think of advice that came at just the right time and steered you in the right direction.

Thank God for all your precious memories. Chances are that once upon a time someone made from scratch a gorgeous birthday cake filled with sparkling candles that you got to gently blow out. Certain people were willing to stay up with you until late hours to greet the New Year. Perhaps you met a beautiful young lady for the very first time and she simply smiled at you.

Thank God for What is Coming Your Way

When you truly commit to attracting what you most want, thank God with confidence for the answer. When you thank God before receiving the answer, you accelerate the manifestation. At times, you will intuit that your wish is perfectly aligned with our Creator's will, and you just know it will be done. This is faith and trust in a LIVING, not dead, God.

Whenever you are in total alignment with God's will, you can have total confidence in its fulfilment. That is when you are in the flow, in full realization that God IS Love, and that you, yourself, are emanating that love. You replace war with peace, hatred with love, despair with newfound certainty.

When you realize God ONLY wants the very best for you, you can begin expecting miracles. Much of our unhappiness comes from doubting that God, and life, itself, wants to give us a break. We convince ourselves that we are unworthy; doomed to failure.

Thank People for Everything They Do for You

Be immediately thankful for even the slightest favor friends and acquaintances grant you. The more appreciative you are of everyone in your life, the more you condition them to do even more. You will find some people who deeply annoyed you in the past suddenly becoming extremely nice to you.

When you appreciate others' consideration, you make them feel very important. Studies of work life show strong evidence that employees want more and more money up to a certain point. However, if they receive no appreciation beyond that, their commitment and satisfaction begin to flounder.

When you remember other people's generosity to you long ago, they will treasure you forever. Often, little things mean a lot, such as giving a glass of water to a man dying of thirst. If you have ever travelled in another country and were invited home to stay overnight with a total stranger, you will know what I mean.

Realize You Can Never Offer Too Much Gratitude

Gratitude is synergistic: the more you give thanks, the more you want to give thanks. When you think of it, gratitude, itself, is one of the things that makes life truly worthwhile. How does it make you feel when others say "thank you" to you? How do you feel when you say "thanks" to others?

Thankful people develop into magnificent people. If you take but a single step every day in being thankful, you will soon stand out from the crowd, and when you enter a room, everyone will sense your presence. It is a little like being with the Dalai Lama, who makes everyone he meets feel like the most important person in all the world.

Thankful people habitually bless others, thereby coming to truly love them. It is as if you are wiring yourself to both say and feel "thank you." When you are thankful for the least possible favor and are thankful to others for the most insignificant thing, you become to others in your world a very special person.

Wake Up with Praise and Gratitude

Start your day with thanks for everyone and everything and praise for the LORD OF THE UNIVERSE. If you reflect upon it for any length of time, it will become obvious that we live, move, and breathe entirely through our Creator. Everyone and everything we see is a gift from Him. Every moment longer we live is but another precious gift from Him.

With praise and gratitude on your lips, you enhance the prospects your day will go well. You acknowledge the Truth behind everything we perceive. We are witnessing our Creator continuously presencing Himself in everyone and everything; a perpetual dance within the Heart of God.

As you praise and thank our Source, you may find yourself becoming divine. We are all extensions of Him, whatever roles we play, whether hero or villain. When we gaze upon Christ as the Avatar of Avatars, we are looking into a mirror seeing ever more clearly what we were meant to be and Who we all ultimately are.

Visualize God's Gift Coming Toward You

See unique blessings make their way to you from our Source. Since He wants the abundant life for you, this is an act of devotion. As Marianne Williams so brilliantly pointed out in *Return to Love*, we run from our own magnificence. To own Who we ultimately are would totally put us on the spot.

People are supremely thrilled when they think that they may be God's gift to you. "God's Gift" is the first name of Europe's most talented musician, Amadeus Mozart. Amadeus truly was the gift of God to higher culture. Likewise, you can calmly own the genius within you.

God, Himself, considers you worthy of all the good He showers upon you. This may be contrary to your religious upbringing, whether it completely denied God or made you an inveterate sinner. Whether you realize it or not, you co-star with the Greatest Lover the World has ever known. The cross was the greatest statement that could be made as to our eternal worth.

Practice Ho'oponopono

Ho'oponopono is one of the most powerful agents of well-being ever devised. "I love you" and "thank you" are the hidden truth behind all human interaction. These words are core to one of the world's most powerful mantras, originated by a native Hawaiian master.

"I'm sorry" and "please forgive me" open the hearts of even the greatest cynics. All you have to do is to keep saying them altogether: I LOVE YOU. I'M SORRY. PLEASE FORGIVE ME. THANK YOU. You can whisper them, think them, or even sing them. Each phrase evokes powerful feelings from our heart.

The effect of repeating these phrases is awesome. They were pioneered by the Kahuna Master, Morrnah Simeona. Her closest disciple, Dr. Ihaleakala Hew-Len, worked with her to spread them around the world. Morrnah eventually addressed the United Nations and was officially proclaimed a national treasure.

Remember

- Gratitude can create a deep feeling of abundance like nothing else. It even beats winning the lottery!

- Thank everyone and everything. Upon inventory, you may find much more than you imagined.

- List thank yous daily for *anything or anyone*. This habit will prosper you more and more.

CHAPTER 12

Aloha: All Is Well

Hawaii is the one US State most associated with paradise. Some 2,300 miles from California, it stands alone in the Pacific with a series of gorgeous islands with the most congenial people you are ever likely to meet. To spend any time there at all is like dying and going to heaven.

In addition to exotic plants and birds, along with its exhilarating trade winds, Hawaii offers a welcoming spirit that instantly promotes well-being as soon as you step out of the plane. You are special for just being there. Residents with the aloha spirit feel very comfortable treating you that way.

Experiencing unconditional love from anyone or any circumstance goes a long way to enabling you to awaken to Universal Love and to begin channeling it to others. While Hawaii may be close to foolproof, you can find other places around the world that lift you up and give you wings to fly.

The Welcoming Spirit

Aloha is the universal word for love, meaning literally, "May our breaths mingle." In Hawaii, it is offered not only to lovers and honeymooning couples, but to everyone. You start by greeting everyone with a smile. Why not? On the islands, visitors are welcome. Residents don't often get to travel more than a couple hundred miles.

In Hawaii, restaurants put gorgeous tropical flowers in the drinks and their food. Why not? There is an abundance of lush vegetation in a climate that can bring as much as 400 inches of rain in a year. Say it with flowers has always been good advice in human relations. In the islands, it becomes spontaneous.

Once you immerse yourself in these gorgeous tropical islands, you adopt a spirit of paying well-being forward to the next generation. Life is precious. You've dropped all pretenses. Love among everyone is cool. You might wish that could be true everywhere. Why not make it so? Why not live outrageously?

Hawaii: The State of Well-Being

Hawaii has preserved the Polynesian spirit of openness and acceptance to an amazing degree. The cool trade winds make these tropical islands especially magical. You don't need heavy clothes. A light sweater or jacket, maybe a feather ski jacket if you venture up to the top of the Maui's gorgeous volcano, Mt. Haleakala, over 10,000 feet above sea level.

Being small islands surrounded by a massive ocean, Hawaiians have developed a culture that prizes visitors who add spice and diversity to their daily experience. We all have a deep affinity with community. Only through visitors can people native to Hawaii feel part of the larger world. Tourists are never to be taken for granted.

With a much slower pace than on the big cities of the mainland, pure being is NEVER taken for granted. For most of us, *just to be* is our greatest accomplishment. Yet, we don't even begin to live until we start being, breath by breath. When we immerse ourselves in a culture that prizes being, we begin to heal ourselves.

Well-Being is a Thriving Industry

Hawaii is a living demonstration of just how much well-being can be commercially viable. When you commit to a higher quality of life, you place a premium on your goods and services. As you produce more consciously, and as you build goodwill into everything you think, say, and do, value and quality take a sudden jump upwards.

Global economic trends point to well-being as the dominant theme of successful business today. Ever since the cultural revolution of the 1960s and 1970s, enterprise has begun to address our needs as total human beings—body, soul, and spirit. Whether Ben & Jerry's ice cream or Tom's of Maine toothpaste, old-world craftsmanship now sells at a premium.

As you prize well-being, you are in synch with what really matters. At some point, quality wins over quantity. Mediocrity works only for surviving, never for thriving. Quality begins by entering fully in the here and now. There, you can experience the inherent perfection of everyone and everything that surrounds you.

Place Your Highest Value on Profound Well-Being

Wellness is vital, but well-being is even more important. For example, well-being is far more than NOT being sick in bed. It is being wholly alive, regretting nothing, looking forward with relish to each successive moment. Well-being is when love, joy, and peace are found to be natural conditions; your birthright.

Well-being implies full integration of body | mind | spirit. When you are always trying to get ahead and beat the system, it is all too easy to sacrifice one or more of these. Many jobs in our digital economy would seem to require only our mind. We can take care of our body after hours, and spirit, well, we can reserve spirit for an hour or two on Sunday . . . if we are lucky!

From a spiritual perspective, well-being is unconditional, flowing out from within. It begins with the breath, the basis for the word "spirit" in ancient times. Until well-being is unconditional, you are always at risk of losing it, even in an Earthly paradise. However, when you center yourself in your heart, centered well-being becomes more and more the norm.

Exit the Squirrel Cage

If you fall in love with Hawaii, you will find that you can always take it with you. You can bring back lots of souvenirs. You can start with your digital camera. Apple's iPhone now automatically starts creating themes for your photos that you can share with friends. Even a conch shell would be sufficient to put you into a vibrant state.

Go out of your way wherever you live to find supportive environments for relaxation, presence, and well-being. In the United States, we are seeing a critical mass of people in every major city and state who have jumped out of the squirrel cage.

Frequent beautiful places within your region for relaxation and enjoyment. When you look at a list of National Parks, it is surprising how many choices we have. Arizona, for example, a desert state, has gorgeous rock formations, such as the Grand Canyon, along with elevated areas featuring ancient Native American ruins. Utah, a neighboring desert state, has stunning rock formations in Zion and Bryce Canyon National Parks. You can also float effortlessly in its Great Salt Lake.

Go Within

As Hawaii inspires its inhabitants to live in the moment, it is natural to go within as much as without. Ultimately, Hawaii is a state of mind; a state of being. In quiet moments, at home or in nature, you can imagine that you are in paradise and trick your mind into believing that you are already there.

Hawaii is a call to fully experience your own experience. Decades ago, the *est* training paved the way for a critical mass of people to stop time and begin to fully experience the now. Every thought is *just* a thought, every feeling is *just* a feeling, and every action is *just* another action. You can get totally high simply on what IS.

Hawaii is a continual reminder to take time out for what matters most to you. Any environment or social context that encourages you to look within to establish your own priorities is a means to stay in touch with your true self. For busy professionals, it may be a simple five-minute stretch where you allow your thoughts to think themselves without your thinking them. You momentarily emerge as the observer.

Just BE

The welcoming spirit inspires you to BE first, and then act. You don't always have to justify how you spend your leisure time. Each of us can find our own secret place, in our own or someone else's garden, where we can breathe freely and feel the sunshine and gentle raindrops. Take delight in each moment as it passes.

Relaxing, taking naps, and going at a slower pace can dramatically enhance the quality of your life. Even from the standpoint of work, more and more of us since the global pandemic are working from home. Whether we had a good night's sleep, or emerged restless, we can recover with as little as fifteen minutes of napping time. This is as much true for youth as for mature people.

When you learn to just BE, you will find you are now free to do anything. You will have ready access to your imagination. You will stop squashing your feelings. Those feelings will begin to power your daily efforts. Your Ultimate Identity contains the entire universe. Why not begin living from that truth?

Contemplate Spiritual Masters

Every morning, spend a moment visualizing masters who learned the art of unconditional well-being. You can focus on an Avatar, Messiah, or Boddhisattva. This is anyone with whom, whenever you see Him or Her, you directly experience God. The more consistently this happens, the more likely you will have heard of them. Krishna, Buddha, and Christ occupy the supreme place, as they have each become archetypal.

You can also focus on saints and sages from all the traditions. The great Ramana Maharshi qualifies as both a saint and a sage. Ramana sat in a cave in total silence for years. Children would throw pebbles at him to see if they could wake him up. Cobwebs even formed around him. Eventually, Ramana woke up, and a small city grew up around him.

You can even focus on contemporary masters and adepts. While it is more challenging to identify true masters without the test of time, it is possible. Baba Ram Dass brought Hinduism to the West in the late 1960s through his master, Neem Karoli Baba. When I first saw him as a college student, Ram Dass was a highly sophisticated psych professor turned spiritual seeker with lots of attitude. Ram Dass remained an icon for decades, even after he suffered a stroke that impaired his speech. Ram Dass ended up spending his days on the gorgeous island of Maui, where he finally emanated the very presence of God, a true saint.

Divine Consciousness: Love, Joy, and Peace

The Christian tradition saw these fruits as growing directly out of communion with God. They were a sign of the presence of Christ. Pure love, pure joy, and pure peace are impossible to fake.

Unconditional Love is THE thing people most want, whether consciously realized or not. Not only we, but the Universe, itself, are a dance of love. Love is our origin, and love is our destiny.

Blossoming Joy is the juice of life, which spontaneously flows out of an open mind and heart. As children, we felt it a whole lot more often before it dimmed away with all the cares of life. Now you can find it within.

Deep Peace without regard to circumstances is the best way to deal with uncertainty. You are never alone. A higher force, a sacred presence, monitors your every breath. Trust in that!

Practice Clearing Process

Every morning, start your day with a process like *Ho'oponopono* that lets your energy flow. Repetition of positive phrases erases all negativity. Those phrases can be in English or any other language, ancient or modern. For example, I like to address Jesus by His Aramaic name, "Yeshua," to which He would instantly respond were He to suddenly appear right next to me.

Consistent use of a mantra cuts away distractions. I remember hitchhiking in the South of France shortly after graduating from Cal Berkeley. I used a simple phrase, "All ways us living love," suggested by the early transformational author, Ken Keyes. I kept repeating it, even while breathing the fumes of leaded gasoline. Even in those challenging circumstances, I got relatively "stoned" with that simple phrase.

Flowing movement, as in ballet and yoga postures, grounds you in your body and immediate surroundings. The more you can dance your way through the day, the more you will capture the gentle rhythm and glide through your chores. When this happens spontaneously, you will be thrilled to see it unfold.

Remember

- Hawaii is ultimately a state of being. The physical state, itself, is close to an Earthly paradise.

- You want to be more than not sick or "well." Well-being lets you be fully alive.

- Your environment continually influences you. It works to go find your own special island.

.

PART 3

Universal Presence

Your Sins Are Forever Forgiven. . .
From Eternity Past To Eternity Future

You most likely are your own worst critic. Even if you are not explicitly religious, you can certainly relate to personal failure, blowing it, messing up. You will never be like the truly great people who live in another world. You have hurt lots of people without meaning to. You have even hurt a few people intentionally when you totally lost it. If there is a heaven, you can't imagine even taking the first step onto the golden pavement.

No matter how bad you think you may be, you are like all the rest of us, both human and divine. No one is really keeping points. They all have enough problems of their own. Even more, you cannot out-sin God's Love. You can't get to the point where your Creator says, "I'm through with you."

As a major nineteenth-century poet, Francis Thompson, put it, Christ is the "Hound of Heaven." He is after you. He wants all of you. Just as you are. He will lose no one. Human love is always relative. Divine love is inevitably absolute.

The Gospel narrative is the greatest force for transformation the world has ever known. The other great traditions have made incredible contributions to humanity. Their founders will always be revered and remembered. However, the Christian faith—as it was meant to be—places an infinite value on everyone with unconditional love that knows no blame, shame, or guilt. The divine love it unleashes is a total mystery. That we cannot always explain that Love doesn't blunt its impact. It penetrates everyone and everything. All we need do is continue moment by moment presencing the Lord of Love. How hard is that?

CHAPTER 13

Deep Listening: Letting God Speak Through the Voice of Another

Few things have a greater impact on our experience and expression of love as does deep listening. When people talk and their partner stops listening, the conversation will rarely be satisfactory. It may be easier to talk than to listen, as deep, conscious listening is an act of creation. By listening, we give another personhood.

The language and words we use to speak are tools that appeal to our imagination, enabling us to realize and act upon the intentions of others, as well as better gauge their feelings toward us.

Most importantly, by listening with our total attention upon others, we can end up hearing God speak through them. When communication is complete, and both parties feel that they have been heard, the Self in them and the Self in us emerges as the same Self. Why wouldn't our Source speak in every way possible to us . . . if we only would listen?

Intentional Re-Creation of Experience

The essence of communication is the intentional re-creation of experience. It is as if one head and heart could pour into another head and heart the full intensity of what they have been through. It bridges the gap between one world and another, creating the experience of "WE."

Words are only tools to that end. They may have originally been grunts and sighs followed by marks on a rock. Over thousands of years, words became almost hypnotic. People came to believe that words and thought had a life of their own. Eventually, we come to today's global society, where people navigate their lives through a sea of words in hundreds of different languages.

When the underlying intention is consciously delivered and mutually understood, we enjoy a sense of completion and intimacy. This is not a function of the number of words spoken, but of how consciously and thoughtfully those words have been delivered. When you speak, it is entirely up to you to see that the listener gets the message.

Observing Silence

For most of us, extended periods of silence are necessary to rehabilitate our ability to listen. In the contemporary world, most of us are continuously bombarded by random messages. We develop an immunity to paying attention to the trivia in advertising, social media, and casual conversations.

We can gradually create a context for communication during a moment of silence. It could be a five-minute break after doing yoga or a long walk in an enchanting forest. It could be deep breathing and deliberately slowing down our pace.

While some people take a two-week solitary Vipassana retreat, silence need not be total for it to open us up to the present moment. Silence in a forest includes any number of enchanting sounds of the leaves whistling, animals grunting, and birds flying overhead singing with each other.

Deep Breathing

When you breathe deeply, you break the ceaseless chatter of your monkey mind. You will find it is difficult to take deep breaths while thinking. As your thought process slows down, it loses its grip over you, and shapes, textures, and colors become more vivid around you.

Breath is spiritual in nature; in some languages, spirit is named after the breath. As people and animals move around of their own accord, they are thought to have breath or spirit. As you breathe deeply, you draw in oxygen that puts a fire into your chest. This metabolic process distinguishes us from plant life.

Conscious breathing puts you in contact with all life. All plants and animals need air to breathe, while fish can breathe oxygen in the water through their gills. It is amazing to consider that this entire planet is alive only through its ultra-thin atmosphere that gives our oceans and skies a delicate hue of blue.

Eye Contact/Body Language

Sixty percent of communication is done, not with words, but with what we do with our body; especially our eyes. Eye contact, along with your body language, signals that you are either open or closed. This process has been minutely studied in the field of kinesics. It can be most profitable in both business and courtship.

Most people pay only superficial attention to body language. We are so caught up in our thought process that we strain ourselves to say the right word. All too often, our eyes and our posture contradict what we would like to express. When our body, posture, and voice are congruent, we are much more credible to others.

You can send signals that deliberately compliment your listener, just don't overdo it. When you have thoroughly studied body language, you can go to a party and read how the people feel. You can quickly see who is most likely open to you. However, if you get too manipulative, the process may backfire. It is never foolproof, and signs can be easily misconstrued.

Open Questions

To deepen the process of conversation, start asking open questions that require something other than a monosyllabic response, such as yes or no. Most people welcome the opportunity to freely speak for themselves. Open-ended questions grant them license to share their experiences much more freely.

When you ask HOW and WHY questions, you make your listener think and disclose more than they would otherwise. Just doing a Q and A around the bare facts is like a legal interrogation or a routine job interview. Nothing inspiring about that. How does she *feel* about various situations in her life?

When you ask others open questions, you increase the probability they will reciprocate the favor. You can develop the policy of conversational generosity. Even when you meet to discuss a problem you are having, first ask your friend what is going on in their lives. While you may occasionally encounter people who are nonstop talkers, most people will avoid taking your attention for granted.

Listening for Possibility

Inherent in language is the power of creation to allow an entirely new possibility to emerge than was planned. Our language shapes what we allow into our lives. We are, each of us, so habituated to set patterns that it is estimated that we have original ideas at most five percent of the time. In order to move forward, we can make the most of these new thoughts and ideas.

Positive vocabulary allows much more possibility than negative vocabulary. When you get upset and scream out what you DON'T want, your subconscious mind ignores the negative word, altering your conscious intention. If you want to change the world, it is much easier to get across what you DO want. Even sophisticated autocrats and demagogues know this, relying upon double-talk.

Deep listening supports others in taking a stand for a whole new level of possibility. It is often easier for our friends, classmates, and colleagues to hear what we are trying to say. When you commit to others living the highest version of themselves, they will often greatly appreciate facilitation. Helping others articulate a powerful new vision is one of the greatest possible things you could ever do for them.

Clean Interaction

Speak straight, self-responsible words without any kind of insinuation or sarcasm. Give your listeners a chance to warm up to you and let you into their heart. It is challenging enough to speak with both clarity and empathy. When you introduce clever put-downs, not only is it a turnoff to others, but it is also genuinely confusing.

Sharp or unkind words and actions almost always backfire. President Donald Trump is an extremely capable businessman and entrepreneur. Donald demonstrated passion, vision, and courage while serving our nation, addressing a host of inconvenient issues that had been sadly neglected. However, his negative campaign with name-calling in 2016 needlessly antagonized millions of people. It came back to haunt his entire administration. Even when a questionable tactic works, you may want to ask if the ends justify the means.

When you speak simply without talking down to your listener, you have a much greater likelihood of being understood. People with advanced degrees are often tempted to dazzle their audience with what they know, including the use of erudite words. In doing so, they run the risk of losing their audience. Clarity beats cleverness every time.

Nothing Left Unsaid

You want to get to the point where your partner feels *nothing* has been left unsaid. As more and more is said between you that needs to be said, the greater the love that spontaneously emerges. Withheld words are often fatal to relationships. They can build up to the point where one or the other party will lose it and say things they will later deeply regret. To prevent this, they can implement paired sharing with a timer, where their partner is not allowed to interrupt until it is their turn. This works incredibly well.

As Werner Erhard, founder of the Transformational Movement, once put it, the truth can be said in less than two minutes. When a share goes on and on, participants are usually getting lost in their story; their version of how things have gone. When they pare down the story to its bare essence and take full responsibility, it gets much more interesting: "I did it, and it didn't work for me."

Once withheld communications are responsibly delivered, true listening opens wide up. Withheld words make trust difficult or impossible. When they are shared cleanly and responsibly, it is often found that they were trivial, and both parties will laugh. You are much bigger than your withheld sentiments. When you let go of them, your magnificence will shine through.

Hearing Between the Lines

When you tune into your partner and sense what they are trying to say, your intuition will often give you accurate information that wasn't explicitly said. You will often sense what your partner is saying before they have completed themselves. This is all part of active listening.

When you intuit a communication, verify it with your partner whenever possible. Occasionally, our perceptions about what is being said will prove inaccurate. If we are on the right track, our partner will let us know and show appreciation. When intuition works, it is often breathtaking.

When you hear between the lines, you can be a more active listener. What is essential is to get to the bottom of what wants to be said. Often, our partner will be confused or frustrated. When you combine both deep and active listening, momentous breakthroughs can happen.

Communion

Deep listening fosters a state of being we could call divine love: You ARE love. I AM love. We all ARE love. We see ourselves in each other, identifying closely. Eventually, we realize that Who we all are IS that Love.

Total communication fosters a very high degree of intimacy. We are all too often preoccupied with survival. It may not be our next meal, but it will often involve getting ahead, losing today in an effort to be in a stronger position tomorrow. Very often this process never stops. When we take time out to listen, we discover what truly matters; what life is all about.

Deep listening is all about creating intimacy with anyone and everyone, not just your family, friend, or lover. It is not strictly a matter of time. Profound intimacy can develop in minutes. Intimacy reveals our ultimate Source: I AM YOU, BEING ME, BEING YOU, BEING ME, BEING YOU.

Remember

- Deep listening is complete communication. You get it, confirm you got it, and confirm they know you got it.

- Sixty percent of communication is non-verbal, and 25 percent of verbal communication resides in the tone of your voice.

- Deep listening is the foundation of real love. You've said everything, and nothing remains unsaid.

CHAPTER 14

Presencing:
Direct Access to Universal Love

Presencing is a word coined by Dr. Otto Scharmer of MIT. Otto works with people, companies, and institutions around the world that are at an impasse. The word means "make present." He formed the Presencing Institute (u-school.org) and created a unique process based on his "Theory U."

Otto likes to ask, "What wants to emerge?"

In any given situation, we can see possibilities that lead to community, harmony, and mutual fulfillment. His process involves having participants systematically release their doubts and fears and go inward. He then leads his participants back out through a prospective project that often results in major breakthroughs.

This process of presencing has been so successful that Otto has offered it at MIT to the entire world free of charge. He trains others to facilitate the process and initiates groups in multiple countries at once. When people become truly present to one another, despite whatever might be going on with them, miracles can happen.

Infinite Possibility is Always Now

We live in an infinite field of possibility that embraces the way it is regardless of circumstances. Infinite possibility allows for the transformation of anything. The way things appear is only the *way they* appear. That which underlies them is *Absolute Unity, Absolute Love,* and *Absolute Perfection.*

You can simply articulate that possibility and hold on to it, whatever ensues. When we come from inspiration, rather than memory, that possibility will begin to grow, slowly crystalizing into what we see as real. The only obstacles are the ones that form in our own mind.

Infinite possibility doesn't depend upon outer conditions. Possibility is a context out of which we live that begins to shape circumstances. As circumstances are continuously shifting, they never need to be a limiting factor. As ancient Hindus put it, "If you keep saying it the way that it is, eventually your word will become law in the Universe."

Time and Distance No Longer Matter
Quantum physics has demonstrated that our communication is no longer constrained by how long or how far. Our thoughts go faster than the speed of light. Think of the planet Saturn, the one with the big rings around it. Can you now visualize it? Whenever you see it, you are there. Realize that this planet is not ultimately "out there."

Our thoughts can transform our past and future in the moment. When you remember your last birthday, it is always now. When you visualize your next birthday, that, too, is now. When you experience any birthday, you always experience now. You are ALWAYS in the NOW. Where else could you be?

Our thoughts can access infinite power in the blink of an eye. Did you ever gaze at an illustration of the Big Bang, when all the stars came into being, starting in a fraction of a second? Where is that illustration? In your experience. Where is the event they represent? In your experience. Is there anything you are aware of NOT in your experience?

Universal Love is Always On
Since Love lies at the very heart of the Universe, it is available right in the moment wherever you are. God's hands are always wide open. If God wasn't everywhere, He wouldn't be available where you are. If there was

any place where God wasn't, this would not apply. Since God IS Love, love is available for the asking.

God is with us every moment of our lives. We aren't always mindful of this, which is to our detriment. Since we *live* and *move* and *breathe* within Him, we can access Him instantly. Just surrender. How hard is it to surrender to infinite, all-encompassing love? Isn't it like going home to everything you could possibly want?

Since God will never forget us, we are assured of immortality. If you think of virtual worlds, using goggles and gloves you can bring them up on a high-powered computer in seconds. Since no less than our Creator imaged us, we can come back in an instant. This may seem a stretch, but it is in accord with contemporary physics and metaphysics.

God is Hard-Wired Into Our Nervous System

Dr. Deepak Chopra, in his classic exposition *How to Know God*, showed just how our seven chakras make the experience of God inevitable. Direct experience of God is totally natural because God is literally hardwired into our central nervous system. If we have need for security, God is there. If we have need for romantic fulfillment, God is there. If we have need for a feeling of boundless unity, God is there.

Humanity was created to experience God within the world of form. God localizes Himself in each and every one of us, so that He can experience our Universe through all of us as us. We take God for granted, much like fish in the ocean take the ocean for granted, as it is all around them.

As we come to thoroughly accept that God *IS* Love, and Love *IS* God, and that God is everywhere and in everything, especially us, we come to realize that we ARE Love. We have direct access to the most powerful force in all the Universe because THAT is what we ultimately are. The avatars and bodhisattvas show us how it is possible.

Invoke the Presence of the Lord of Love

When you recognize the Avatar, or Christ, for who He is, you can simply call Him to experience Him. Invite the Lord of Love in, as He is already knocking at your heart's door. You can simply try this out. Invite Him in, regardless of how bizarre it may seem. As you keep inviting Him in, suddenly you will find that He has walked into the very center of your heart.

As you presence Christ, He begins to speak and act through you. This is the entire basis of Christianity. All the rituals, doctrines, and theology point to this. As you align with Christ, you progressively become divine. As you share this with others, you help provide them access to experience this for themselves. What else could it be but a miracle that Saint Francis of Assisi took this so far that he received the stigmata, or the very marks of the crucified Christ, on himself?

As you experience Christ, you will find yourself totally at home. The big lie is that your Creator means you ill. Why else do you suffer? If you think Christ doesn't care about you, why would you ever want to call on Him? Think of the serpent in the garden. He could only work through doubt. When you begin to truly TRUST God, that sneaky snake slithers away.

Surrender to the Lord of Love

When you feel that Presence, you will automatically open up to Love. Love is surrender to the Lord of Life. Albert Einstein posed the question, "Is the Universe friendly?"

After many years pondering this, Einstein maintained that this was the most important question he ever asked. The answer is, "Yes." The very moment you consciously FEEL that Presence, it will be clear.

The more you surrender, the more you will realize we live in a divine love story. When you watch a romantic comedy, you often forget you are watching it, as the dramatic tension seems so real. You don't always realize that "all's well that ends well," and comedies, by definition, have a good ending. Is it not intriguing that Dante Alighieri chose the word "comedy" for his masterpiece epic poem, *The Divine Comedy*? When all roads ultimately lead to paradise, how could he call it a tragedy?

As you keep surrendering, you will discover the Lord of Love to be your only True and Ultimate Self. If you suppose you are your body, it won't likely seem immortal. If you are your mind, you may increasingly grow forgetful. If you are that which animates your body and mind, then you truly are a reflection of spirit, or the "breath" of God.

Allow that Which IS to BE

When you let anything else be, it lets YOU be. As fear is driven from your heart, you will allow whatever IS to be. We both fear and desire the unknown. As we come to realize that the unknown will increasingly give us what we desire, our resistance to it eases up and we can dance through life. Whatever is, IS.

Werner Erhard's original *est* training showed people with undeniable clarity how they could experience whatever is, recreate it, and have it give way to something entirely new. Your experience is *your* experience. It is not really "out there." It is actually "in here." When you begin to own your experience, the world will open up to you in daring new ways.

You will soon find that you are no longer confined to the way it is. You will enter into the flow, where the world is ever new, just as you will never find any two snowflakes exactly the same. You are a creator within your own creation. You have no need to hold on. Trust the flow.

Experience Your Divinity

Recognize yourself as an incarnation of the Lord of the Universe. Once you own your divinity, you will become fully human. If God is everywhere, then He is in everyone and everything, *including you*. To be fully human is to be both a creature AND the Creator in one individuality.

The Creator, Himself, lives within you. As the Anglo-American philosopher, Alan Watts, put it, "You are an aperture [portal] in the Universe."

God, as the Universe, experiences the Universe from your unique vantage point. You will never be ultimately fulfilled until you realize that God is your only True and Ultimate Self.

As the Creator, you are eternal. As a human being, you appear to be mortal. However, what is truly YOU about "you" is your divine nature.

Since each of us, in the eyes of our Supreme Self, is infinitely precious, that Self can remember each of us at any time He chooses.

Recognize that it's Not Your Love, But God's Love Through You

When you feel divine Love, you will realize it to be God flowing through you. All you have to do in the words of Father Thomas Keating, founder of Centering Prayer, is to "consent to the Presence of God." It is a little like seeing all of us in a gigantic party yet feeling God within and underneath it all. Since God IS Love, He cherishes us, as each of us is indispensable to the total expression of that Love.

Allow yourself to channel that Love. Every time you see, hear, or feel someone, think of that person with appreciation, blessing, and forgiveness. This is all the more relevant if that person is an opponent, or especially if you see him or her as "The Enemy." Love the person anyway. The feelings will come as you persist in this.

Keep on channeling that Love every morning, day by day, week by week, month by month, year by year. Eventually, your whole world will be transformed. You will have only magnificent people around you. You become magnificent as you fully acknowledge the magnificence of others. No one can resist this Love for long.

Come into Life as a Son or Daughter of God

You will finally realize your mission as a channel of THAT LOVE which is God to everyone and everything. As you begin to consciously fulfill your mission, you will find Who You Are to be invincible. Sure, you may get upset and lose your composure or your perspective. However, your divine Self will spontaneously spring back.

As you gaze at others, you will find that you are surrounded by God. You begin to see not just with your eyes, but with your heart. As you become more and more willing to see the highest version of those surrounding you, it will begin to come true. It is an amazing process!

You can then enter your daily life from a position of utter triumph. This Love ALWAYS triumphs, even though things might get uncomfortable for a bit. People want nothing more than to have others love them. To resist that Love when it is pure is utterly demoralizing. People will eventually realize that they are only fighting themselves!

Remember

- Presencing is the ultimate secret of the Path of Love. Since God is everywhere, Love is everywhere.

- Invite the Source of Love into your heart. You will find Him already there, the express image of our only True and Ultimate Self, Universal Love.

- We live in a field of Infinite Possibility. LOVE is always to be found because the entire Universe lies within that Love.

CHAPTER 15

Gandhi Today:
How We Can Continue His Work

Many people consider Mahatma Gandhi the greatest man who ever lived after Buddha and Christ. When Richard Attenborough released his epic biopic, *Gandhi*, he swept the Academy Awards, winning eight separate awards, including Best Picture. The film created a global context that within several years helped end the intractable Cold War, helping humanity breathe easier for decades.

Gandhi started as a timid, awkward young attorney who could barely present a case only to emerge as the most powerful leader of the twentieth century. Eknath Easwaran wrote the classic analysis, *Gandhi the Man*, showing how Gandhi pulled this off during a fifty-year period with all the odds lined up against him.

Gandhi's shocking secret was simply that he followed Christ's "Sermon on the Mount" literally, not with just a handful of people, but with millions of his fellow patriots. He practiced *Ahimsa* (non-injury) relentlessly, actively loving the very British who subjugated his nation for centuries.

Did it work? Gandhi, more than any other human being, brought down the entire British Empire, the largest our world has ever seen. He loved the British to the point where they couldn't help but love him back. Many Nobel Prize laureates closely followed his example, including Martin Luther King Jr., the Dalai Lama, and Nelson Mandela. The Mahatma did all this without lifting a finger toward violence.

Satyagraha: Hold Fast to the Truth

Satyagraha is the Sanskrit word coined by Mahatma Gandhi for grasping the Truth no matter what. Regardless of external conditions, we can always take a stand for the Truth. The Truth goes beyond the news of the day and the bare facts. The Truth touches on our inherent divinity and the all-pervasiveness of God.

The Truth is that we are all one, each a reflection of the other. Whatever our race, national origin, gender, or religion, we are in essence one being with many faces. Diversity is to be welcomed and highly valued. Can you imagine the monotony of us all being literally the same person? More to the point, the same Self gazes out of each one of us, the Light of Supreme Consciousness.

You can stand for the Truth while respecting all sides of an issue. For example, many people died from the recent COVID-19 epidemic. However, people dealt with it in different ways. The issue of boosting your immune system, which makes a whole lot of sense, was sidelined in favor of masks and mandatory vaccines.

Ahimsa: Nonviolence

Ahimsa is the Sanskrit word Gandhi adopted for his standard of interaction: non-injury. Violence can apply to thought, word, and action. You may not injure someone physically while still seething with hatred, which is highly damaging on a subtle level; damaging not only to the recipient, but to the one who releases such low vibrations.

You can even harbor violent thoughts without articulating them. If you deplore the actions of someone, you need not bad mouth that person. In recent political controversies, President Trump comes to mind. You either loved him or hated him. Much of the mainstream media chose to assassinate his character, rather than dispute his actions.

You have the power within you to surrender incipient violence in your mind or heart through love. If you focus your attention on love, itself, it is difficult, if not impossible to hate someone. Love is a function of relationship, rather than some kind of power play. Heal the relationship, itself. Then the actions will follow.

Channeling the Power of Love

When you open up to divine love, you will find that you can direct it towards anyone or anything. With practice, you can continually send thoughts of love to difficult people. For the better part of twenty years, I have prayed daily for every president the U.S. has elected. I found that I developed the greatest bond with the more challenging presidents. Somehow, they seemed all the more human.

Since love is what we most want, the people to whom we offer it will eventually reciprocate, even though it might take quite some time. Life throws us into opposition with others, whether in sports, business, politics, or even the military. This opposition should not determine regard for our opponent. In a tennis match, you are going to enjoy a much better game when played all out than if he or she played against you only half-heartedly.

You will find channeling love vastly more effective than attempting force. When someone slights you, they expect you to react in kind. When that fails, they begin to wonder, even question themselves. When you have high regard for them, you need not agree with them, just see the validity of their viewpoint.

Radical Inclusion

Gandhi treated everyone he was with as supremely important, regardless of caste or social status. As Jesse Jackson put it, "Red and yellow, black and white, we are all precious in His sight."

When the Mahatma was a child, his priest read from both the Bhagavad Gita and the Holy Qur'an. In a predominately Hindu country, Gandhi went out of his way to protect the Muslims.

When your thoughts and actions start including everyone, you will discover an irresistible force. Many people at various times may attempt to dominate, but when you have deep regard for them, their antagonism will melt and they will feel vulnerable. At that time, reach out to them with the greatest love.

When everyone is included, all things are possible. In South Africa, Nelson Mandela went from being a political prisoner to president of the nation. Rather than seeking revenge on the very people who made him break rocks, he chose to go all in on the white rugby team and rallied the Blacks in that support. South Africa ended up winning the Rugby World Cup, weakening the hold apartheid had on the country. Clint Eastwood, in his deeply moving film, *Invictus*, portrayed this story in an unforgettable way, with Morgan Freeman playing Nelson Mandela.

Honoring Indigenous People

Today, the indigenous people of every continent are the most marginalized. When we honor our indigenous brothers and sisters, we honor the Earth. Earth is our mother in a very real sense. Indigenous people's senses are attuned to every pulse of creation. In disregarding the Earth in an attempt to dominate and master it, we have disregarded them.

We need guidance from the people living off the land as much as they need us. Of course, without the land itself we would all perish. Indigenous people know all about a low carbon footprint. They can hardly think otherwise. As Chief Seattle put it, "Man did not weave the web of life. He is merely a strand in it."

Indigenous cultures typically place a high value on Truth, and thus nurturing relationships. All too often, in dealing with White settlers, the Native Americans found those settlers spoke with "forked tongues." Treachery and deceit are ultimately self-defeating. As we begin to emulate our indigenous brothers, we will mature as human beings and become a blessing, not a curse, to our mother.

Interfaith Movement

As Gandhi deeply honored people of many different religions, so can we. Each religion reveals a piece of the Face of God missed by all the others. For example, Islam does the best job of conveying the ultimate majesty of the Creator. Hinduism best shows us how God is in everyone and everything, and thus it is all divine. Christianity reveals God in relationship; that God is Love, itself. As quantum physics reveals, reality and life are defined by interrelationships.

Interfaith strengthens, not negates, the faith of our fathers and mothers. We begin to define our own faith by the careful study of other faiths. We soon find that we don't really leave our childhood faith as much as enable it to mature to perfection. With the vastness of God and the Universe, there is room for an endless array of perspectives.

A universal outlook is what can save humanity from self-destruction. The United Nations was heavily influenced by the Baha'i faith. Baha'i temples are built so that each religion can walk in through a different door. Their ideal is one language and one God. With new technologies, such as Google Translate, we all can share a single language. With a unified understanding of the great spiritual traditions, we can deeply appreciate one God; that one God is all there is.

Citizen Diplomacy

Gandhi never craved public office because he was able to change the world simply by being a totally responsible citizen. Today, more than ever, due to social media and networks, ordinary people can turn the world upside down. With smartphones and tablets, along with Wi-Fi networks, people can make the news in just a few minutes through the power to both document and broadcast events in real-time.

Do you know that every call you place to a political leader counts for 10,000 votes? Ask yourself how many people in your community call the White House at least once a week? Yet our president keeps a voluntary team at the White House to continuously monitor the pulse of the public. I have seen a response in the newspapers within twenty-four hours of my comments. Trust me. It is never a waste of time.

Nations and states are, in the end, just people like you and me, multiplied many times over. Most of what you have thought, felt, said, and done is shared with millions of people around the world. We are all human, be we a billionaire in a limo or homeless person begging for quarters on the street. Powerful people are often quite alone, subject to the same doubts and concerns as the rest of us.

Going Viral

Psy's video, "Gangnam Style," with one billion views on YouTube, caught the attention of the UN. The ambassador of South Korea recruited him, a mere entertainer, to be a spokesman for South Korea! No politician could get that many views! It takes less and less today to win your own "fifteen minutes of fame," as Marshall McLuhan put it.

Are you able to act outrageous in a positive way? Way back in the 1960s during the Civil Rights movement, a group of Native Americans seized the opportunity to occupy a former federal prison on the island of Alcatraz in the San Francisco Bay. As this was regarded as federal government property, their dramatic action did much to boost awareness of their rights both as Native Americans and as US citizens.

Thinking outside of the box is increasingly prized. Steve Jobs called it "connecting the dots." He was the first person to see that computers could become consumer electronic products for the masses, and Apple Inc. became the greatest company the world has ever seen. Elon Musk is making a comparable play in the aerospace and automotive industries.

Gandhi's Moonshot | Our Moonshot

A moonshot, as defined by Singularity University, is to *positively impact one billion people within ten years.* Just as it took less than a decade to put men on the moon, any one person or group can initiate a movement that can impact almost everyone in the world. Today, you can release a video, audio, or text file that can potentially touch that many people.

If Gandhi could bring down the entire British empire through love, and that is how the British eventually regarded him, what *can't* we do with today's technology? Today, it is possible to organize a twenty-four-hour meditation around the world with people assembling in every time zone, all connected by smartphones.

When you give love away to as many people as you can, you often get a massive return on investment (ROI). In 1965, Swami A.C. Bhaktivedanta, founder of The International Society for Krishna Consciousness (ISKCON), arrived in New York with $60 in his pocket. He commenced building Krishna temples and giving away free food. Within a decade, he had these temples all around the world! In doing so, he catalyzed the spread of Hindu culture globally, including in America. Today, many first-generation Americans born in South Asia are providing leadership here in the United States at the C suite level in Fortune 1000 companies.

Seeing the Highest Possibility in Everyone

When you wake up to the infinite potential of every human being, you will be surrounded by love. Buddha could see the highest potential in this incarnation of everyone he met. He formed his own society, eliminating barriers of caste, educating them in the art of being. In the process, Buddha transformed much of the world, including all of East Asia.

President Nelson Mandela bet his office on bringing out the highest potential of Blacks and Whites. You might say he was "colorblind." He just saw people. He put Whites and Blacks equally in his cabinet, refusing to give preferential advantage. In addition, he launched the Reconciliation Movement with Archbishop Desmond Tutu to heal the deep wounds between the two races and compassionately address all the grievances between them.

When you glimpse your own highest potential, you will be awed by our collective magnificence. If you don't optimize what you do, we don't optimize what we do. Your contribution, however small, is priceless. No doubt, you have any number of talents you have placed on the back burner. It is high time you reviewed them and tried something new.

Remember:

- Gandhi consistently held fast to the Truth while unconditionally loving all his opponents. *So can we.*

- Gandhi treated everyone he met as if they were the only person in all the world. *So can we.*

- Gandhi easily impacted directly or indirectly one billion people for good in his last years. *So can we.*

CHAPTER 16

Telling the Truth to Power: Fight Back with Love

Three questions are often given to test whether what you say will stand the test of love:

1. *Is it true?*
2. *Is it kind?*
3. *Is it necessary?*

Saying the truth to others in an insensitive way flunks the test of love. Even if the thought is both true and kind, it is sometimes not expedient. It may not be what those in power need *at that particular time.* For example, an American president will often have to make a decision demanding total concentration that will impact millions around the world. I can think of John F. Kennedy and the Cuban Missile Crisis.

There are times, however, when your insights can contribute to those in power if you simply give up making them wrong and see things from their perspective. Working in sales for decades, I have learned the hard way that "the customer is always right." You don't make a sale by being a jerk.

In the case of President Trump, he was unsure whether to meet with the President of North Korea, Kim Jong-un. I phoned the White House and urged him to go ahead. Our relationship with North Korea had deteriorated to a dangerous level. I saw that, whatever you might think of him, President Trump had passion, vision, and courage. He was just the man to deal with Kim. The rest is history.

Everyone You Meet Your Mirror

I am I only in so far as you are you. South Africa's *Ubuntu* shows how each of us defines everyone else. You are completely necessary for me to define myself. I need you every bit as much as you need me. We are all members of an intricate web of mutual interdependence.

Your True Self is all of it. You are everybody, as everybody is you. All apparent differences are part of the fun and make life endlessly fascinating. What you identify with as yourself is your piece on the board game of LIFE. Without your piece, and that of every other player, there would be no game.

Your body and mind orient you to the playground you have created. You inherently belong here, as does everyone else you meet. We needed a world as our playpen to play together, even as the world, itself, needs us as players. In truth, no one and nothing is out of place.

Support Alternative Networks and Media

Since mainstream media often distort situations, alternative media provide the counterbalance. Facing open censorship and extreme paranoia, you can respond to the beat of a different drum. As both mainstream and social media attempted to muzzle President Trump, they inadvertently suppressed us all and invited the formation of competitive media that might honor privacy and everyone's right to speak freely.

Media worldwide have been increasingly consolidated and may no longer represent you. In the United States, six major conglomerates own the majority of brands. Not just newspapers and magazines, but TV networks and film studios. It becomes increasingly difficult to speak up and out with integrity.

When you get thrown out of one network, go look for another. If we monitor the extreme actions of Facebook and Twitter in throwing out a sitting President of the United States, it becomes clear that they also dishonored the millions of people who stood by that President. Rather than being a conduit of information, of late, they have become a political weapon. You can be sure they will eventually generate their own opposition. For example, Musk has bought Twitter with the claim that he did this to restore free speech.

Befriend Your Opponent

Your opponent will often be stunned when you befriend him. You can play the game with ease when you place a premium on sportsmanship. Kindness makes for a far better game. When on the court, play all out. When off the court, give more thought to how good the game was and less thought to who won it.

Your opponent ultimately is there to bring out the best in you. He or she is doing you a favor. Have you ever tried playing tennis all alone? The best you can do is bounce the balls against the wall. The only justification for that exercise is to prepare to play a real game. The game, itself, is the reward.

Every single one of us is worth understanding; each of us has a unique story to tell. *YOU* and *YOU* and *YOU*! Some of us had a smooth upbringing, and others a very rocky one. A few of us have spectacular achievements. All of us have had to deal with constant obstacles, upsets, and reversals. All of this is intrinsic to the Great Story that we call Life.

Align with the Opposition

When you adhere to the truth and loosen up your position, you can get in step with the opposition. Even if the opposition seems determined to walk off a cliff, you can approach them with compassion and love. Each of us does what we feel to be right at the time. As we are constantly learning, we can always profit from other people's experiences.

If you feel smugly righteous, chances are you stand to learn a lot from the other side. This is true of Creationists versus Evolutionists, Democrats versus Republicans, and Fundamentalists versus Humanists.

The more we learn about, and from, the other side, the more love will spontaneously emerge between us both.

President Lincoln started out as a brilliant attorney who could articulate his adversary's case better than they, themselves. He thus defeated many of the advocates of slavery both intellectually and politically. In military strategy, few things are as important as to know your "enemy" and to never underestimate him.

Reveal Present Unworkability

Show the other side what isn't working without making them wrong. When things aren't working well, your opposition is not very happy. Why try to make him even more miserable? Give him a chance to make it work. Gandhi mastered this. He would stop a campaign when he gained the advantage. His intent was not to beat the British, but to enlighten them, which he did with consummate style!

When you are 100 percent responsible, it is never the other person's fault. The moment you stop blaming your opponent, you can begin to create a true win-win situation. In 2022, Russia launched an all-out campaign to annex Ukraine, using tanks, troops, and bombs. That military campaign has backfired in that it has inspired worldwide opposition. Why punish all of Russia because of the rashness of one leader? When Ukraine suffers, Russia will also. Our opportunity is to show Russians the way out of this tragic dilemma.

Hold to the essential truth while asking the other side for their perspective. We all want the same things, including and beyond, shelter, food, water, and basic comforts. The other side has a different view in how to obtain them. That is all. Actively show them a better way to obtain what they want. Remember, violence is always an expression of weakness.

Suggest New Possibility

For every A or B, you will find a C that opens another course of action. Since each of us holds a different piece of the puzzle, why not play together? For example, during the COVID-19 pandemic, the dominant rhetoric was around self-protection, even if all human values had to be forfeited: social distancing, masks, and vaccines. What if boosting our immune systems took front stage in the debate? Basic vitamins and minerals have been demonstrated to make a difference through the work of professional nutritionists and physicians. By focusing on C as a possibility, we won't feel so victimized.

Possibilities are as open as the one who asks the question. How you formulate the question shapes the answer you get. Whenever a question leads us all to a dead end, start asking new questions. It goes back to the quote of the late Robert F. Kennedy, "Others ask, why? I ask, why not?"

Ask input from your adversary. It is worth considering that *Playboy Magazine* once sent a black journalist to interview an American Nazi. Their conversation was most intriguing. While the Nazi espoused his racist theories, those theories were progressively undermined by the creative discussion of a conspicuously intelligent African American.

Uphold Friend and Foe Alike

Make it your job to uphold everyone, starting with your perceived foe. When you uphold your foe first, it throws everyone for a loop. Throughout Gandhi's amazing career, it would look like he was an agent of the British, having received his legal training in London. It pays off royally to act like a lady or gentleman.

A foe is a friend that you haven't yet come to know. The opposition usually comes about over our very ignorance of what the other person is thinking and feeling. When you let him know that you believe in him, whatever his opinion may be, it opens the space for a more creative discussion. Everyone is right in their own eyes. The enlightened value love over being self-righteous.

Since unconditional love is what we all want most, start giving it. You can never go wrong. American presidents have kept ordinary citizens in their "kitchen cabinet" simply because those citizens were never mad at anybody. When you think about this, you realize that good humor is a very precious quality.

Positive Politics

When you arrive at a fork in the road, go for the positive side. The positive is infinitely more powerful than the negative. To differentiate the positive, we need the negative for contrast. However, the negative is always subordinate to the positive. As the New Testament maintains, He who is within you is greater than he who is without.

When you stop reacting to the negative, you make your opponent question himself. Like little children, we often rebel simply as a means of getting attention. Give people the attention for which they are starved by concentrating on their whole being, not their momentary temper tantrum.

Positive politics is characterized by a quiet confidence that has no need to prove itself. We get derailed whenever we try to prove ourselves. An outstanding track record usually speaks for itself. Smart politicians throw the attention on the audience, which is what the audience cares most about.

Run for Office

Try running for office without making your opponent wrong. When you truly love your opponent, you melt their resistance. During President Trump's heated debate with Hillary Clinton, a brilliant member of the audience submitted the question, "What do you like about each other?"

Trump complimented Hillary on her persistence. Against all forecasted odds, Trump then went on to win the election.

When you want your opponent to win even more than yourself, you garner unprecedented support. Way back in 1992, the billionaire, Ross Perot, was virtually drafted into running for president, starting with an interview on TV. Perot evinced dissatisfaction with both major parties while showing little overt ambition. The audience and the broader public went on to fall in love with him. Perot then decided to run for election and actually won five million votes, most of which would have gone to President Bush. President Clinton, who gave us the internet, subsequently won the election on a plurality.

In running for office, even if it is for president of a local club, you learn to respect your opponents for the courage it took them to run. Even if the other person is blinded by personal ambition, it took them a lot of courage to run. Most people choose the easy path of never taking a stand.

Appeal to Love Over Fear

Fear and hatred are expressions of weakness; faith and love are expressions of strength. When others insist upon the path of fear and hatred, you need not buy the ticket. It is noteworthy that Laurene Powell Jobs, widow of the late Steve Jobs, actively opposed President Trump's wall along the Mexican border. However, she had previously taken the time to personally visit with him.

When you love friend and foe alike, you become a hero in their eyes. Here, Jesus Christ takes center stage. The very Pharisees who gave Him such a hard time in His earthly ministry ridiculed Him all the while He was suspended on the cross. He looked up and asked, *"Father, forgive them, for they know not what they do."* (Luke 23:34)

Subsequently, Christianity became the world's largest religion through the initial efforts of another Pharisee, Saul of Tarsus, who, as Saint Paul, declared Jesus as Lord across the Roman Empire.

Since love is what we all most long for, why not start with it? Think what people will do for the glory of an Oscar in Hollywood. To address a billion people across the planet and to enjoy the adulation of hundreds of millions is rare, indeed. However, your ultimate triumph begins by loving the very people who surround you, starved for that very Love that has fed Christianity for 2,000 years.

Remember:

- Everyone you meet is your mirror. Welcome to eight billion YOUs.

- Align with your opponent, show him unworkability, and suggest positive alternatives.

- Live in possibility. Choose faith and love over fear and hatred. Give up being right.

CHAPTER 17

Final Exam: Transforming Your Worst Enemy into Your Best Friend

With this chapter, we come to the heart of *Waging Love*. If you can consistently love your enemies, you can get a gold star and start teaching others in the School for Love. If you can truly get behind this chapter, then we all have a chance of realizing the moonshot of giving a billion people direct access to Universal Love. Imagine one billion people who can instantaneously channel a love so divine that it has overthrown empires.

The key is to realize that your worst enemy is a huge opportunity for which you must be profoundly grateful. He can deliver more insights to you than anyone else. You can immediately decide that he is NOT your enemy. Making someone an enemy is always a choice. You will find that choice never serves you. You can consistently send him love using everything you have learned. Realize that no one takes joy in fighting true love. This is never what an enemy expects. If you keep sending him that love, you will soon inspire him to become your best friend.

If you only knew the power within you, you would burst out laughing, crying, and sprinting up and down the street. This comes from realizing that it is not "your" love, but that LOVE which IS GOD that kisses your enemy and brings him to your arms to sob for forgiveness. It is your precious opportunity to BE CHRIST to your world.

"We Are All Such Sinners"

Toward the end of his life, Gandhi articulated the utter futility of judging anyone else. When you own and accept your own failures, you will do so for others. As he put it in Richard Attenborough's classic film, *Gandhi*, "We are all such sinners, it is up to God who goes to heaven and who goes to hell."

When you discover God as pure Love, you will have no interest in counting points. You will permanently exit the judgment game. Since God IS Love, then hell is but the absence of God. This is clearly impossible. That Love, which IS God, is impossible to resist. The hardest criminal will crumble in the face of such love.

The greatest sinners often make the greatest saints. It defies all common sense that Saint Paul was initially the greatest opponent of the early Christian community. On the road to Damascus, a center of the early church, Paul, as Saul of Tarsus, saw a great light that blinded him. He heard Jesus ask him, "Saul, Saul, why do you persecute me?"

In the wake of this transformation, Saul of Tarsus as Saint Paul did more than any other human being to put Christianity on the map, writing much of the New Testament.

Rascal or Scoundrel? Join the Club

We are all either scamps, rascals, or scoundrels. In the light of the cross, heaven has room for us all. We are all naughty in one way or another. It is only a matter of degree. Scamps are a delight. Rascals are a challenge. Scoundrels are all but impossible. Transformed by that Love, all of these creatures become saints.

Whereas before you would get upset meeting another rascal, or especially a scoundrel, soon you will burst out laughing. We are all just being human, and occasionally, animal. However, who we really are is the Creator within His own creation. We have all forgotten this and await the transformation of Universal Love.

You can be both magnificent and petty at the same time, which appears to be a total contradiction. When I did the original *est* training decades ago, they taught us this. It seemed so counterintuitive. Yet, when you accept being petty, you can accept being both. Too often, we hide from our Divine Self, convinced we are totally unworthy.

Your Worst Enemy is a Matter of Perception

How you see things draws the limits to your compassion. Enemies are not "enemies" unless you say so. We all consciously have a set of rules and expectations. When another violates them, even family, we begin to separate ourselves. Yet what we see "out there" is but a mirror of ourselves within.

A Course in Miracles reveals that a miracle only requires a shift in perception. When you begin to realize that every single person you meet is a son or daughter of the Living God, you begin to look again with fresh eyes. Surprise! When you look for their divine Self, you will find it.

Forgive Him Verbally

It greatly helps to simply speak out the words, "I forgive you."

In turn, it is appropriate to ask for your own forgiveness, as well. You can even do this mechanically if that is what it takes. Somehow, those very words have the power to induce an open state of love. Forgive them AND forgive yourself, which is often much harder to do.

Keep forgiving and blessing your enemy until you actually feel that way. If you are like most of us, you may need to resort to forgiving individuals every day. It will slowly dawn on you that taking offense at others is a total drag. Much of what you see in them is in you to an even greater degree.

You are never very far away from the expression of God, of Absolute Love. This may seem easy to say, but impossible to do. Etty Hillesum, a Jewish lady from the Netherlands, died during World War II in Auschwitz forgiving and blessing her Nazi enemies. She was not the only one. While Etty forfeited her life, she died a true saint.

Bless Him No Matter How You Feel

Blessing your enemy is the fastest way to experience that you have no enemies. Every morning, without fail, bless your worst "enemy." I have practiced this for nearly twenty years, praying for presidents I initially loathed and countries that seemed out to destroy America.

You will soon find that they are becoming your best friend. For example, I prayed for certain Republican presidents, simply invoking a divine blessing upon them. President Reagan became totally transformed, brought an end to the Cold War, and actually hugged Mikhail Gorbachev. Every time he made any kind of peace initiative, I called the White House to thank him. I was stunned by the results. It went so far that finally, even Soviet generals toured American bases!

You will find that time and space are no obstacle. You can invoke blessing upon characters who are long gone and see them in a different light. If your opponent is on the other side of our planet, no problem. As you experiment with this long enough, you will be utterly shocked at the results. You will find that IT IS ALL WITHIN YOU.

Discover the Miracle of Love

Watching his guru channel miracle after miracle, Ram Dass came to know the true miracle. You will soon see that this Love has no limits. Ram Dass's guru, Neem Karoli Baba, could walk through locked doors and appear at multiple places at once. Yet these phenomena were nothing compared to the bliss his devotees experienced at the master's feet.

You will watch this miracle transcend the past, the present, and the future. This Love is eternal. Above all, the Christian tradition offers Eternal Life. What few followers grasp is that eternal life is in this Love. This Love IS eternal. God IS this Love, and so, ultimately, are you and me.

In this Love, you will discover everything you need to know about God. Your world will be metaphorically on fire with glory. It can lead you into total presence, where you can stop time and enter the timeless. It is the "Pearl of great price," where the jeweler sold everything he had to buy this one pearl.

Nothing So Bears the Interest of the Son of God

The Gospel discloses how forgiveness is the road to "joy unspeakable and full of glory." (1 Peter 1:8-9) The fastest way to be like Christ is to forgive like Christ. Life is set up in such a way as to give us abundant opportunity to forgive others and ourselves. We keep forgetting who we all are, relying upon misleading impressions.

Why not play a different game? Why not compete in helping others realize their true magnificence? It is in every one of us, if only the sheer apprehension of a human being. We are all angels in the making, enrolled in a school for love where we have yet to learn the language. Patience. Just a little more patience.

Your worst "enemy" is a gift to you, just as you are to him. Years ago, Robert De Niro played a bounty hunter against Charles Grodin in *Midnight Run*. Robert had to take Charles to the authorities to collect his bounty, and Charles kept slipping away from him. Amusingly, Charles was a "white collar criminal," but without perspective, Robert was intent to put him behind bars. At the end of the film, Robert realized Charles was his guardian angel!

No One Can Long Resist

If you focus on showering your enemy with love, he will melt right before your eyes. It is truly tough to resist pure love. Since we all tend to be highly reactive, your enemy counts on you resisting him. That way, he can get points by commanding your attention. When you totally accept him as he is, the game is over. He needs no points to win your love.

Soon, the resister will feel like flipping over to your side. What he really wanted all along was some form of love, as twisted as that may be. Hate, itself, is a very distorted form of love. Only indifference is the true opposite. You have now given him permission to love others back in a pure way. It is much easier than trying to cause trouble.

Invite your enemy to join you in transforming our world. For example, environmentalism, whether it is air pollution, the population explosion, global warming, or climate change, was politicized by Democrats, such as

Al Gore. As time continued, many Republicans also became appreciative
of the issue. They became part of the solution, rather than part of the
problem. It is a great mistake to make any one party the center of all evil.

Bring Entire Nations to the Negotiating Table

What is true for individuals is equally true for nations. Be a love ambassador. You may live in a major metro area where you run into people
from every country in the world. This is a huge opportunity. Many of
them will still be first generation, traveling back and forth. By being
kind and loving, you subtly contribute to world peace.

Anything you do for a citizen of another country strengthens your
own country. This is true even if their country has become a technocratic
totalitarian surveillance regime. Behind this wall of oppression lies real
people susceptible to the power of Love. When it hits a critical mass, this
Love can go viral. Your own country will be all the more safe and secure.

Every day, bless every nation you see as difficult. If you continuously
read the mainstream news, you will likely spot plenty of problem countries that you would never care to visit. See this as an opportunity. Even
though it may seem futile to transmit goodwill to despotic regimes, this is
never the case. Given the principle of nonlocality in physics, every impulse
of goodwill within you is instantaneously transmitted across the world.

Study God's Problem Countries

Every country has a story and is worth understanding, just like each of
us as people. When you understand the history of nations like Russia
and China, you will find many of their actions make sense, even if they
are not to your liking. You have the power within you to transform
international relations.

As you bless entire countries and their leaders, something shifts in
the larger world. We keep coming back to the ultimate truth that other
people are within you, just as you are within them. The entire galaxy
spins within the context of our Absolute Being, which is none other
than whom and what we call "God."

As a son or daughter of the Living God, you have infinite power at your disposal. You just need to catalyze that power by invoking the Sacred Presence. Let that Presence start flowing through you and begin to channel it toward any difficult or problematic issue. From this perspective, this Earth can be seen as a playground for us to grow up into the full measure of our divinity.

Remember:

- We are all scamps, rascals, or scoundrels. It is only ever a matter of degree. God smiles at us.

- Forgive everyone all the time. It works to even say the words out loud, "I forgive you."

- Pure Love is irresistible. It is utterly demoralizing to fight against that Love.

CHAPTER 18

Divine Lover: How to Become Who and What You Truly Are

We all live in a divine love story, continuously playing out in the mind and the heart of God. Each of us as actors are uniquely precious expressions of the ONE. We are so blessed that God settled on a love story rather than a monster movie. Love stories are happy stories. Despite all appearances, life is more a comedy than tragedy. Best of all, it is not over until it's over.

In case you haven't figured it out, *YOU are the star, along with the Lord of Love.* Jesus Christ, as the ultimate hero, provides an unforgettable model for who you truly are, as well. You have the power to transform your world, because your world lies within the ultimate context of your being. You get to wake up your fellow actors from central casting. You wake them up with nothing less than true love . . . infinite, eternal, and absolute.

If you look at your world today, you will most likely see infinite ways to radiate love for everyone and everything. Awoken beings have been in the millions, possibly even billions. You may be convinced that you can never rival their accomplishments. You don't have to. The game is all about being surrounded by divine beings all the time. You don't have to be great yourself, you just need to keep seeing the greatness within them.

What to Do Until the Messiah Comes

Depending upon our upbringing, we either fear or long for the Second Coming with intense emotion. We no longer need wait for the Kingdom, as we can bring in the Kingdom now. Just as Christ's disciples couldn't envision His resurrection happening in advance, so we don't have a true grasp of what His return will look like. We can bet that it will be stunning and truly glorious. However, we can make the Kingdom more real each and every day of our lives.

When we eventually become who we truly are, we will find Christ all around us. Just as Christ was chosen, and shares with us an eternal destiny, so each of us is also chosen. We are all uniquely powerful versions of what we see in Christ; a new humanity/divinity. Despite all appearances, *homo sapiens* are being transformed into Divine Beings.

The Second Coming is the destiny not only of Christ, but of all of us. The transformation that Jesus Christ demonstrated in His own life will become the destiny of every single one of us. All are forgiven. All are redeemed. It was never up to us, but our Creator. We await the Lord of Love as a bride for her groom. In the face of Universal Love, no one and nothing will be left out. God's love, like the sun, is totally impartial.

No If, But When

We no longer need to wonder *if* we will become Absolute Love, but *when*. Since the cross, the outcome is no longer in question. Each of us learns to love our fellow humans as the Master loved His early disciples. The moment you realize that everyone is infinitely precious, you have passed the final exam.

Since the Love of God is eternal, we will all awaken to that Love sooner than later. The joy of life is to have that awaken among all the people in YOUR world. You become that Love so that you can spontaneously project that Love to others, who in turn project that Love to still others.

God is not forgiving for just some of the way, waiting to clobber us the next time we fail. God is forgiving ALL the way. That is the whole point. We are all brothers and sisters of a single, transformed family. Jesus Christ is the perfect image of what will happen to us. In a way, each of us can do no wrong. "Right" and "wrong" are a matter of judgment. We are not here to judge but to love unconditionally.

You Already ARE Love

When you cut through all the sham, you will find that Love is your very nature. When you know yourself as Love, leading a miraculous life becomes a compelling option. Nothing is so empowering and powerful. No one knows what to do with that love but to surrender in kind. Those who resist that Love have an utterly miserable time. They will melt faster than you can imagine.

Even when you act like a total scoundrel, Love is who you really are. We all have our favorite enemies, people we would gladly assign to hell as totally unredeemable. Being a scoundrel is also a miserable state to be in. Give people enough time and they will wake up and try something different.

Emperor Ashoka was responsible for the deaths of tens of thousands of soldiers in a neighboring state when he attempted to subdue them. There was so much bloodshed that Ashoka was utterly disgusted with himself. Out of this disgust, he became a Buddhist who enshrined nonviolence throughout India. Ashoka even went so far as to export Buddhism around the known world of his era.

When you realize there is ONLY GOD, and GOD IS LOVE, you suddenly discover why you are here. You are cast in a movie whose overriding theme is Love; Divine Love. Whatever happens is ultimately alright because it is all part of a glorious love story. When you get with the overriding agenda, you can start having a splendid time. There is only a happy ending to this type of story.

Cut Through Your Pretense and Shadow

Ask how much your pretense is costing you, and if it is worth it. As soon as you recognize that you are a sinner, you will discover that you are also a saint in the making. We can't have a saint without a sinner, and the greatest saints are often the greatest sinners. It won't take long before you truly crave emerging as a divine human being.

When you start forgiving everyone in your life, don't forget yourself. You should not be surprised by now that you, yourself, are the hardest person possible to forgive. Why? Because you are always with yourself, but not always with your worst enemy. You know all your creepy, selfish, petty, and mean thoughts. Who would possibly forgive YOU?

We are all perpetual students of Love, and the grace available to us is infinite. How could you create a story of the triumph of Faith and Love over fear and hatred without plenty of dark moments? A hero requires a villain. A story requires suspense. Most often in our story, it looks like we won't make it. That means it is the perfect story. We fool even ourselves.

The Less of You, the More of God

As you begin letting go of all you thought you were, you will discover an angel fluttering in the wings. You are an infinitely precious localization of God. Every blossom and flower is gorgeous in its own right, however short its life. However, the flower doesn't know that it appears as a flower when it is really God, Absolute Unity | Absolute Love | Absolute Perfection. In contrast, you can know.

God wants nothing more than to free you of delusion. That is His role in the drama. Life in the world we are in seems the only thing that is real. That this is all in the mind of God is hardly ever realized by the player. The whole point at any point in the play is to wake up to the power and presence of Love.

When God declares you innocent, nobody and nothing will ever contravene it. God only sees who you truly are, *inherently* divine. What you do with it is only part of the story. Jesus Christ made it abundantly clear in His Sermon on the Mount that God is not into judgment. Neither should you be. God's joy in this story is to bring everyone back home. That means YOU. Not just the person sitting next to you. YOU!

Feel Divine Love Surge Through You

The greatest joy in life is to feel Divine Love flowing through you. You will never find anyone who couldn't use more Love. Then give people what they really want. It starts out so simple with the words, "I love you."

These words don't even need to be spoken out loud. With sufficient repetition, they evoke the requisite feeling. People subliminally pick it up, even when they are on the opposite side of the world.

As you consistently channel that Love, you will never run out of it. Love is infinite, eternal, omnipresent, and omnipotent. Just like God. In fact, this Love IS God. When you are filled with this Love, you are filled with God.

Whatever your circumstances, you can always offer Love. A thank you. A smile. A quiet blessing. A word of appreciation or admiration. Eventually, it will become a habit. Where you initially are highly selective, more and more you will freely offer it to everyone and everything that comes along your path. This Love is home. When you are truly at home with yourself, you are totally free.

Stop at Nothing Less Than Divine Love

Nothing but Divine Love, itself, can save the world. Divine Love is Universal Love for a reason. Personal, romantic love is a wonderful warmup. However, you soon find out that it is conditional. It will only take you so far. When you surrender to a Higher Power, a more powerful Love will take over from there.

Universal Love transforms all resistance into Love. Like the flowers and the song of the Beatles toward the end of the animated film, *Yellow Submarine*, the "Blue Meanies" are utterly defeated. Everything is swept up in a perpetual spring. This Love comes from the core of your being, a direct reflection of who you really are.

Since you are already divine, offer the world the Divine Love within you. The only price you pay is to continuously presence God. You have been mindless for so much of your life, now is the time to practice LOVE.

It begins with simple words, as used in Ho'oponopono: I LOVE YOU. I'M SORRY. PLEASE FORGIVE ME. THANK YOU.

Your Destiny as an Embodiment of Love

When you recognize that job number one is to embody Love, you will find it easy to set your agenda. This love is freely available to anyone for the asking. When you run into a real character going out of his way to give you a hard time, laugh and smile. Keep presencing God moment by moment. No need to take offense.

Love abides deeply within you. When you are being irresponsible or pulling back from life, you only need surrender and open up to who you truly are. You never have to look outward to find this Love. Jesus spoke about His Spirit being given to His students. That Spirit is like an exquisitely elegant flame that purifies and transforms everyone and everything in its path.

As pretense and shadow slowly drop away, you will find only the Love of God. Remember the childhood game of hide and go seek? We all learned this well. When tagged, "You're it!"—you have to go find your playmates, who are doing their best to hide from you, much like Adam and Eve in the Garden made themselves scarce from God after eating the forbidden fruit. Of course, we are all eventually found. But this is a big part of the fun.

"For YOU So Loved YOUR WORLD That. . ."

The greatest verse in the Gospel (John 3:16) talks not only about Christ, but also about YOU. Were you fully in touch with Who you are, you would have freely done what Christ did. It is utterly painful to walk about where no one knows who you are, nor do they even know who they are. You would do anything to wake them all up. Christ is the one person who already did and became the ultimate Hero.

Since that work is forever complete, you can live out of the context of that Love. Christ is the Way Shower. All we need to do is remember and follow His example, being powered by His Spirit. The Lord of Love is the Lord of the Universe made visible. When you call Him, He will respond, as He already dwells in the nucleus of your very being.

The stage is set: You are the greatest Lover YOUR world has ever seen! Everyone's world is unique. However, each of our worlds is interlinked with all the others. When you open all the way and become a truly great Lover, others in their worlds will follow suit.

Conquer the World with That Love

Christianity conquered Rome because it unleashed a greater force than the Empire had ever seen. Your destiny is to conquer your world through that very same Love. You may feel you are not even remotely up to the task. Are you reading this? If so, it is a sure sign you are ready. Precious few people ever get even this far. Know that it is not YOU, but the LORD OF LOVE within you, that will pull this off.

You will be a hero to the degree that you see everyone around you as truly magnificent. When you are out of touch, they will hardly seem magnificent. However, when you are deeply in touch, you will see the divinity within them sparkle, just waiting to come out. It is your job to bring out the divinity of everyone you meet.

As a son or daughter of the Living God, own up to ABSOLUTE UNITY, LOVE, and PERFECTION. When you get totally clear that there really is NOTHING BUT GOD, you will begin to look past appearances into the heart of reality. We are all one. God IS love. We all are, as well. In a state of surrender, everything is perfect, just the way it is, AND it can be any other way, also. We live in a world of inherent perfection. You are in heaven already, and you don't even know it!

Remember:

- You are already a son or daughter of the Living God. It is only a matter of time before we all see that.

- Great people only have magnificent people around them. Transform your perception to transform your reality.

- The Love that conquered the Roman Empire can transform your present world into paradise. That same Love dwells within each of us as our only True and Ultimate Self.

Direct Access to the Lord of Love

The time has come for us to take this mission, vision, and message out into the world. You can start with family and friends, neighbors and colleagues, and then anyone you meet. It begins with your thoughts and feelings. You can direct it all inwardly. Eventually, you will find yourself acting outwardly. As you continue moment by moment, day by day, it will begin to permanently impact your world.

Christ gave it all away in a single sentence, showing us **the Way, the Truth, and the Life**. (John 14:6) When you awaken to that Truth, you will find the Way and the Life along with it. God is Absolute Unity, Love, and Perfection. The Way of Love is the Perfect Path to God. The outcome is a Divine Life supersaturated with Love, joy, and peace. Supreme ecstasy and bliss. Is anything more important to you than that?

Your potential is no less than to BE CHRIST to a world hungry for His Presence. You will find that This Love will NEVER let you go. Do you now see that it is entirely possible to awaken the world in a single generation? You will never be truly satisfied without a burning mission, vision, and message. Why settle for anything less than the highest version of YOU in this very lifetime? We are all awaiting the moment you join us in this ultimate dance of Love.

The Way, The Truth, and The Life

The night before His crucifixion, Christ identified Himself as *The Way, The Truth,* and *The Life*. Until now, most people have yet to fully understood these words. His apostles may have taken it merely as a personal statement. All but one forsook Him when the power structure of that time came down on them. Later, fundamentalist Christians would use these very words to browbeat anyone who refused to acknowledge Jesus as God.

To the degree you, yourself, fully grasp these words, you will transform the world. I AM IS The Way, The Truth, and The Life. I AM is the most sacred name for God in the Hebrew tradition. We all share like Christ I AM as our only true and ultimate identity. Jesus' name in Aramaic means "I AM salvation," which suggests, "I AM transformation." Each of us has the power within us to totally transform. Jesus Christ is the gateway to that miracle.

Contemplating these words will reveal the glorious Love story you co-created with our Source. As Jesus Christ makes God visible to anyone who has the incomparable privilege of beholding Him, He is the Living Word. As such, He co-created the Universe with the Father and the Spirit. He now extends that privilege to us, to join Him as the Living Word. As Saint Paul put it, whenever we identify with Him, we become His body, made visible to all the world. A new humanity. A new divinity.

The Way: Universal Consciousness

The way to transformation is to awaken to the divine perspective. You may call it awakening, enlightenment, realization, or being born again. Only with the advent of the new physics have we as humanity been totally clear that the Universe as such, and everything within us, is not ultimately real. We see and feel form. Matter is but a concept. In truth, all is spirit. All is God.

You suddenly realize that the Hindu concept of God, *Universal Being, Consciousness,* and *Bliss,* is all there is. The Christian equivalent is *Light, Life,* and *Love.* The physical intermingled with the biological intermingled with the divine. We, ourselves, have no identity apart from God. With God, we become a uniquely precious localization that can be brought back to life at any moment.

141

When you realize that you ARE that Consciousness, you become one with everything and everybody. When you come home to your true self though the resurrecting power of Divine Love, you become one with everything and everyone you see. You are inside them, just as they are inside you. It becomes an exquisite play, a divine play, or *Lila*, as the Hindu tradition calls it.

The Way: Universal Love

Universal Love is the way we all directly experience God. Divine Love is impossible to resist. While there is the way of knowledge, action, and contemplation, only that Love can take us behind the lions of paradox and contradiction, behind the final curtain to the inner sanctuary of our Source. Divine Love always knocks at the door of our heart. As military lore has it, "There are no atheists in foxholes."

Divine Love is the theme of the story we find ourselves enacting. As the Greatest Story, it has many twists and turns. We find reason to doubt. Yet we sense, despite all appearances, somehow it will all turn out well. A love story can be a funny TV series, like *The Big Bang Theory*, or a glorious romance, like *Shakespeare in Love*. Since our Creator has exquisite taste—look at the infinite complexity all around you—it will in all likelihood be more like Shakespeare.

Divine Love is the very power that chases away any fear that could stop us. As Saint John wrote in his first letter, "Fear has torment." When the Lord of the Universe is madly in love with you, how could you fail? If you want a string of breakthroughs in your life, keep asking, like Tony Robbins does, "What would I do if I knew I could not fail?"

As Saint Paul summed it up, "He who spared not His own Son, but gave Him up for us all, how shall He not with Him, freely give us all things."

The Way: Universal Presence

Since God is everywhere, God can be accessed by anybody at any time under any circumstances. To experience irresistible love, presence the

Lord of Love. When you fully realize that all love ultimately comes from Him, and He is madly in love with you, you will fall madly in love with Him, and dare to be the greatest lover in YOUR world.

You simply presence the Lord of Love by calling on His name: YESHUA in Aramaic or JESUS in English. If you don't yet see Him as the Lord of Love, open your heart to the highest manifestation you have experienced. It could be *Mother Mary*. It could be *Buddha*. It could be *Krishna*. Each name has a psychic signature. You can demonstrate this by your very own experience. This is way beyond some play on words! Try it.

As you let the Lord of Love enter you, you will find that He is already there. Where else could He be? Since you also are inherently divine, He is most readily found in the sanctuary of your heart. The "He" could, of course, also be "She." The more I study the life of Christ, the clearer it becomes that He is both masculine and feminine; fully human, fully divine.

The Truth: Absolute Unity

Despite any appearance to the contrary, we are all ONE. Recognizing our unity is the fastest way home. We are pearls in an infinite necklace; strands in an endless web. Each pearl, each strand, reflects all the others. Eventually, we arrive at the full realization that there is only ONE of us. And that ONE we call GOD, the Lord of the Universe.

Coming from unity will make life, in the words of Helen Keller, "a daring adventure." No one promises you it will always be easy. However, you have the power within you to make it truly glorious. It is possible to play all out in this wonderful dance. If everyone and everything is inherently divine, you can honor them as such, even the very bugs that crawl up your leg. The world is alive. The universe is alive with the Lord of Light, Life, and Love. It is enough to make us want to dance and keep on dancing forever!

In unity, you will see God's hand has been resting firmly on the steering wheel all along. When it all seems utterly futile, you might resonate with William Shakespeare, "Life is a tale told by an idiot full of sound and fury, signifying nothing." But if you step far enough back from the day-to-day drama, you will see it all as the Divine Comedy; the Divine Love Story where you have an indispensable and unforgettable role.

The Truth: Absolute Love

Love is not merely an attribute of God, LOVE IS GOD. Love is how God feels. Theologians may disagree, but on this, Lovers are of one accord. If God IS Love, then Love IS God. Pure Love = Pure God. If you want more love in your life, more love to give to others, then go back to God, go back to Christ, go back to any of His living expressions, and commune with Him. This is the most real thing you will ever know. Just do it!

The glorious feeling of Love makes it all worthwhile. We often get this in a peak experience that validates our life. It can literally be climbing a mountain top. It can be extreme sports. It can be an exquisite moment in creating great art, music, poetry, or dance. At that moment of grace, everything seems to flow. Go with it. Remember it when you seem to forget.

The Way makes this feeling a practical reality day by day. There are many practices in many different religious and spiritual traditions. Choose what most speaks to you. *Ho'oponopono* is a great way to start: I LOVE YOU. I'M SORRY. PLEASE FORGIVE ME. THANK YOU. Over and over, you repeat it. Address it to whoever or whatever concerns you. Ultimately, address it to your Higher Self, your One and Only True Self.

The Truth: Absolute Perfection

You are perfect because your God, who IS the Universe, is perfect. When nothing looks perfect, you can shift your perception to realize that everything is perfect. If you sensitize yourself, you will observe a delightful, fascinating, and breathless inner pattern in everyone and everything. The grossest madman cannot utterly succeed in defacing it. As badly as we abuse our Mother Earth, nevertheless, she is still there.

Perfection rests not in what you do or don't do, perfection rests in who you truly ARE. Perfection is in WHAT IS. The world of form mirrors the inner world of being, consciousness, and bliss. While totally relying upon our monkey mind, of comparison and contrast, of judgment and evaluation, we couldn't be perfect for even a single moment. Stop the mind. Get off the merry-go-round. Then you will, in an instant, intuit the perfection of it all.

You needn't cling to this realization, as it will most certainly return again and again and again. Life is a process of becoming complete, and then feeling incomplete. Becoming complete, feeling incomplete. Like tomorrow's sun, the experience of perfection is sure to appear on the horizon. Just keep opening up to it. As the incomparable Steve Jobs put it on his deathbed: "Oh, wow! Oh, wow! Oh, wow!"

What a perfect response to life!

The Life: Irresistible Love

The payoff of following the Way is to realize the Truth and enjoy a life of irresistible Love. You are now clear where to look to find this Love. As you focus more and more on the Lord of Love, whoever that might be for you, the more you will find yourself becoming like Him (or Her). It is the ultimate love affair: ME becoming YOU becoming ME becoming YOU.

You look outwardly to see the Lord of Love in everyone you meet. The miracle is in how we see it all. The Christ is latent in every single one of us. Due to the very nature of the living play that we find ourselves enacting, not all of us have awoken. As Ram Dass once put it, "The snake sheds its skin at the rate it sheds its skin."

No rush. It will all eventually happen.

You look inward to see the Lord of Love permanently at home within you. If God dwells within you, where can you go? God is everywhere. How much easier to close your eyes and commune with Him. This is the ultimate reward, to come home and go back to Being God, moment by moment by moment. As you keep doing this, you have the potential, like the early Christians, of turning your world upside down!

The Life: Irrepressible Joy

According to the Apostle Peter, abiding in the Truth leads to "joy unspeakable and full of glory." As you experience God everywhere, in everyone and everything, you realize the Abundant Life. Christ declared His mission, "I have come that you might have life, and that more abundantly." This joy can drive you out of your gourd. You can skip and hop along the road in sheer joy! It is utterly irrepressible.

The greatest joy is among lovers, and you are becoming the greatest Lover in YOUR world. We invite you to join us in the moonshot of moonshots: In the next decade, enable one billion (1,000,000,000) people to become the greatest Lover in their lives, in their world. Just because it has never been done doesn't mean it is impossible. Never before in the history of humanity has there been so many people all at one time hungry for Love, joy, peace, Universal Consciousness, Universal Love, Universal Presence, Absolute Unity, Absolute Love, and Absolute Perfection.

The joy of being fully alive has no preconditions. Some people awaken through a near-death experience. Others awaken through a love affair that burns a perpetual flame in their innermost being. Finally, others awaken through a transformational training. They are eventually led to stop clutching to their limited self and open up to receive their Universal and Ultimate Self.

The Life: Incomprehensible Peace

Hanging out with the LORD OF LOVE leads to a peace that defies all reason. The traditional Near Eastern greeting, for both Jewish people and Muslims, is "Shalom!" or "Salaam!" (Peace!) because there has been so little of it. We try to make peace after waging war and find it doesn't work so well. Only absolute surrender does the trick. However, waging love opens up all possibilities. How can anyone wage war against someone else who is waging a love campaign for him or her?

When you realize that God IS that peace, you no longer feel like resorting to blame. God is in you. God is in your neighbor. God is in your enemy. God is in whoever you meet along the way. Just acknowledge God as soon as you see Him, wherever you go. When you start seeing Him in everyone, there is no one left to fight!

When you fulfill your highest calling, you will be an irresistible peace agent. Our Creator deemed that all of us are needed to complete this incomparable Love story. If you feel God can't get it right or has a warped sense of humor, think again. All God requires of you is that you play all out, and that you look into a mirror and remember who you are: The express image of the Eternal, Living God.

Divine Lovers Throughout Time

You will find profound inspiration from some, or all, of the enlightened beings on this list. Many of them in their time were not all that different from you. A couple of them may still be alive today. Several of them, such as Buddha, Christ, Muhammad and Gandhi, have changed the face of the world forever, making God-realization possible for all of us. Millions of people throughout history and living today have awoken in both their head and their heart, committed to honoring each of us as infinitely precious sons and daughters of the Lord of the Universe. This list is your invitation to join them and make the moonshot of Universal Love over the next decade a reality.

LORD KRISHNA

Lived: 1000 BCE (Could be much earlier)
Country: India

Why Krishna: Lord Krishna is regarded by hundreds of millions of Hindus as the supreme Avatar or descent of God. Krishna demonstrates an irrepressible joy, ease and mastery of life in any circumstance. He reveals the ultimate purpose of Life, that it is all God at Play (*Lila*). Play is a big secret to Love.

Message: We are all God, despite the infinite variations between us. God lies within all of life, even plants and animals. God is our only True and Ultimate Self. The goal of life is to come to the full realization of God. The Gita points the way through several different paths. We come to realize that our Eternal Self lives forever.

Source: *Bhagavad Gita* (Many versions. Most famous: *Bhagavad Gita as It Is*, by Swami Prabhupada) (Book)

LAO TZE
Born: 571 BCE
Country: China

Why Lao Tze: Lao Tze authored the *Tao Te Ching*, one of of the greatest books in any language with just eighty-one brief chapters. Lao Tze goes to the heart of life, ignoring the endless machinations of society, focusing on the natural world of creation. We can know the Creator by pondering His creation. Love is learning to let go. Flow with the river. No need to swim upstream.

Message: The whole point of life is to follow the mystery of things with unabashed wonder. Our little selves are simply part of the fabric of life. As we allow anything to be, it lets us be. Everything we could want is to be found right here, right now. Relish the miracle of life as long as you are here.

Source: *Tao Te Ching*, (Many versions) (Book)

SIDDHARTHA GAUTAMA (THE BUDDHA)
Born: 563 BCE
Country: India

Why Buddha: The Buddha invented enlightenment as an institution. His metaphor was awakening from sleep. Buddha is literally "the man who woke up." His preoccupation was the elimination of suffering, which he felt was caused by attachment, or clinging, to one condition despite inevitable change. The impact of his life and message is incalculable. It formed the basis for much of East Asian civilization with hundreds of millions of adherents through the centuries. Buddha became the ultimate exemplary of wisdom and compassion.

Message: Eliminate suffering for yourself and others through the realization that this life is ultimately a dream. When you give up any and all attachments, you are finally free. The joy of life is to be wholly in the moment while allowing it to be whatever it wants to be.

Source: The Buddha (Video), David Grubin

Jesus Christ
Born: 4-5 BCE
Country: Judea under the Roman Empire (Israel)

Why Christ: It has been said that Christianity IS Christ. The word "Christian" means "Christ in us." The world's largest religion and a spiritual foundation of Western Civilization is wholly focused on becoming Christ, or a son or daughter of the Living God. Christ is best perceived as *the* Lord of LOVE, where God IS LOVE. To see Christ is to see God. To see Christ in anyone is to see God in them. We are all inherently divine, even when we fail to realize it.

Message: God loves you with an absolute Love, greater than a father and mother for their son or daughter, greater than your best friend. God loves you as your only true and ultimate lover. God would do anything for you, and He already has. He has gifted you with eternal life in that LOVE. As you love everyone around you, your inner Christ becomes visible to the whole world. Our only race need be as to who can love us all the most. As you make others magnificent, your own magnificence begins to shine.

Source: New Testament (Four Gospels) Many versions: *New King James, The Message (Book)*

Mohammad the Prophet
Born: 570 AD
Country: Arabia

Why Mohammad: In the establishment of monotheism as the world's dominant theology, the faith that Mohammad, bless his name, inspired, Islam, was the decisive factor. While the Roman Empire had already been converted to Christianity, it gradually lost much of its power. Rome had been overtaken by Germanic tribes, and Constantinople, today Istanbul, had limited power and control. While Jewish people practiced in synagogues, Rome had long before destroyed their temple. Within 100 years of Muhammad's death, the Arabs built an empire that reached from Spain to the borders of India. Over the centuries, Islam developed a religious culture and civilization superior economically, politically and militarily to that of Christian Europe. Only the invention of the steam engine in England in the year 1712 turned everything around. Despite recent confusion, doubt, and cynicism, Muhammad lived a pure, devout and holy life that has continued to inspire hundreds of millions all around the world. Evidence suggests that Muhammad's repeated encounters with God were authentic. His book of divine recitations, *The Holy Qu'ran*, is second only to the Bible in global impact. An impartial study shows Islam to be a very democratic faith with historically high standards for women and children. Every *sura*, or chapter, of the Qu'ran but one proclaims that God is both merciful and compassionate. Any apparent allusions to hell comprise a small minority of verses. Most surprising to many is that Muslims hold Christ as the greatest of prophets. They accept the Virgin birth, the ascension of Christ into heaven, along with His eventual return.

Message: There is no god but THE GOD (Allah). Ultimately, there is NOTHING BUT GOD. We in no way can prosper or find fulfillment by ignoring God. To fully awaken to the infinite power, presence and knowledge of God is to become enlightened. We are the highest form of creation, uniquely capable of fully appreciating God. We must remember Him as much as we possibly can. We are all children of God, who forgives us of all our sins. His compassion and mercy are inexhaustible. We therefore must forgive, love and care for our neighbor as ourselves, regardless of race, religion or nationality. There is to be no compulsion in matters of religion. God has revealed Himself throughout history in many different ways. The whole point is to honor, worship and celebrate the One God, Creator of us all.

Source: *The Message*, by Mousteyan Akkad (Video) and *Muhammad: A Story of God's Messenger*, by Deepak Chopra (Book)

Saint Francis of Assisi
Born: 1182
Country: Italy

Why Saint Francis: Saint Francis has been called the Second Christ. While starting out life as a lay man, he immersed himself in the gospels and so identified with Christ that he received the stigmata, or marks of the crucifixion. What followed was an unparalleled Love, giving everything away, embracing poverty, kissing lepers, exalting women and befriending the Muslim Sultan, regarded by the crusaders as the enemy. Most of all, he loved plants and animals, even the sun and moon, calling them brother and sister. Believing in the One God, Saint Francis saw That God in everyone and everything.

Message: Worship and celebrate God in everyone and everything. Seize every day to make another step to being like Christ. Forgive everyone and everything. Devote your life to being a continuous blessing to everyone in your world. The Prayer of Saint Francis has been a classic unequaled in the history of Christianity. It focuses on becoming an instrument of Divine Love.

Source: *Brother Sun, Sister Moon* (Video), by Franco Zeffirelli

Jalal al-Din Rumi
Born: 1207
Country: Afghanistan

Why Rumi: Rumi has become the most popular poet in America, despite having passed on centuries ago. Rumi became a superstar through the masterful poetry of Coleman Barks, a disciple of the Sri Lankan Sufi Bawa Muhaiyaddeen. Through his poetry, Rumi became an archetypal lover of God through his encounter with Shams of Tabriz. He literally fell off his camel! They entered into a devout communion that allowed Rumi to directly experience God, rediscovering Islam through his heart. His talent in poetry enabled him to communicate that love to humanity.

Message: God is our ultimate Lover. While we can love God through others, we always find they are only instruments of God. Each of them is like the moon, while God is the sun. The Qu'ran reveals that God is closer to each of us than our jugular vein. We can whirl our way like the dervishes in pure celebration of being. We wake up only when we fully realize there is ONLY GOD. Islam employs the term *"fana,"* meaning annihilation. When we dive into God, nothing is left of us but God.

Source: *The Illuminated Rumi*, by Coleman Barks and Michael Green (Book)

Dame Julian of Norwich
Born: 1342
Country: England

Why Dame Julian: Julian is one of the greatest of saints, a revolutionary female mystic who survived the plague that killed up to 50 percent of the people in Europe. She wrote the first surviving book in English by a woman, *Showings*, insisting that God is more like a woman than a man, both our "Mother" and "Lover." Julian came close to death at the age of thirty, having a series of visions over a day or two that utterly transformed her. She clearly saw that "all shall be well, all shall be well, and all manner of thing shall be well." This line was quoted verbatim by T.S. Eliot, the greatest poet of modern English in his *Four Quartets*. Curiously, seeing Christ, she heard no mention of hell. Julian was utterly consumed by His Love, as shall we all be.

Message: You may have total confidence that we all live in a divine Love Story. In the darkest hour, all shall be light. God is Love, and no one and nothing can stop that Love. To experience your greatest well-being, simply focus on that Love. This Love rules over life and death. It transforms everything it touches. We thus have no one and nothing to fear. This Love is ours forever.

Source: Showings of Julian of Norwich, A New Translation (Book), by Mirabai Starr

William Shakespeare
Born: 1564
Country: England

Why Shakespeare: William Shakespeare may be the greatest poet in all of history, the father of modern drama, and even of modern English. Before Shakespeare, English as a language was overshadowed by Latin and French in the royal court. England had not yet risen to the pinnacle of world power that it would two centuries later. Hundreds of words and expressions we use every day are borrowed directly from his work. Most importantly, Shakespeare gave the best depiction of romantic love ever written with his play, *Romeo and Juliet,* which shows how romantic love, when it is divine, is eternal.

Message: All the world is a stage, and we are its actors. We are here for just a scene or two, and then are promptly escorted offstage. Life is a celebration. Enjoy life to its fullest through Love, itself. Only Love gives us immortality. When we love well, we will be remembered through our very love. All the rest is up to God.

Source: Shakespeare in Love (Video) by John Madden

Mary Baker Eddy
Born: 1821
Country: United States of America

Why Mary Baker Eddy: Mary was a pioneer in introducing spiritual (or mental) healing to the world. She did this without the need for any physical contact. As a philosophical idealist, Mary regarded the world with its senses as ultimately an illusion. God is All in All. Since God is Perfect Love, everyone and everything is that, as well. Mary had a stunning ability to spontaneously heal people all around her through an overwhelming love. She saw that we are all whole, complete, and perfect. As we realize our perfection within, that which is without conforms to our purified vision. Mary cured every kind of disease, including broken bones, without even touching the subject. She resuscitated several people from certain death. Mary founded a global church with a definitive textbook for reading the Bible metaphysically. Mary was, for all intents and purposes, the founder of the *New Thought Movement*. As a true prophetess, her influence upon humanity is incalculable.

Message: Divine Love always has, and always will, meet every human need." Christ, as the embodiment of that Love, can be invoked anytime, anywhere. His healing power can become our healing power as we commune with Him. Christ is the Way Shower for what we all can become. We thus live in infinite possibility.

Source: Science and Health with Key to the Scriptures, (Book) by Mary Baker Eddy

SRI RAMAKRISHNA
Born: 1836
Country: India

Why Sri Ramakrishna: Sri Ramakrishna may have been the closest to the Divine we have seen in humanity since Saint Francis, Mohammad or Jesus Christ. He saw God in everyone everywhere. Although the presiding priest in a gorgeous temple complex devoted to the Mother Goddess, Ramakrishna once called himself less than the dust of a servant's feet. He even cleaned a public bathroom with his hair. Without extensive education, he stunned the intellectuals of Calcutta with his wisdom and grace. Ramakrishna underwent stringent tests for true enlightenment and came out surpassing anyone's expectations. He began to search all religious and spiritual paths, finding God in each of them. He even had the experience of merging with both Muhammad and Jesus Christ. All the while, Ramakrishna stayed very human with a lively sense of humor and an energetic body graceful in both dancing and acting. He was passionate about the unity of all faiths through Vedanta, the metaphysical philosophy that all is ONE. Ramakrishna went on to inspire his disciples to share this vision of Unity with the world. Swami Vivekananda, his most talented disciple, travelled all the way to America, opening up the world's first Parliament of Religions with his classic brothers and sisters of America speech. Swami Vivekananda, the first fully enlightened sage on American soil, was immediately met with a standing ovation.

Message: Everyone tells time by his own watch, assuming it to be the true standard. All the religions of the world are but our best attempts to come to terms with the Eternal Mystery. Since there is ONLY who and what we call "God," everyone is a uniquely precious localization of that Mystery. As we love, serve and remember God, we begin to see Him in one another. God is at play in the Universe through us. We each play different roles: beggar, billionaire, refugee, president and pop star. Some of us are considered saints, others sinners. Behind and within each of us is the very same God. Our duty in life is to both fulfill our *dharma*, our proper role within society, and to realize God through whatever practice appeals to us. The greatest honor is to awaken humanity, both individually and collectively, to its own divinity. We are all uniquely precious children of the Living God, whatever our race, religion, nationality or gender. No need to fear the future. Your Heavenly Father has your back!

Source: *Great Swan,* (Book) by Lex Hixon

MAHATMA GANDHI
Born: 1869
Country: India

Why Gandhi: The Mahatma was the first man in history to successfully apply Christ's *Sermon on the Mount* on a massive scale never before dreamt possible, ultimately freeing India from the grip of the British. His efforts directly led to the conversion of the British Empire into the British Commonwealth. Gandhi did this, first in South Africa, where Indians were a minority, and then in India, itself, where the British were a minority. His key was *Satyagraha* (holding to the truth) and *Ahimsa* ("noninjury in thought, word, or deed"). Out of his love for ALL humanity, Gandhi loved even the British occupying his country. He literally loved the British out of India and right back to their homeland. Gandhi did this without money, position, or overt power. Everyone around him was susceptible to being converted to his way of thinking and being. Many scholars compare him to Christ.

Message: Any person can accomplish what he has accomplished if you simply pursue your goal as totally as he did his. Even if only one man agrees, the Truth is still the Truth. The arc of history bends toward justice. You can change history by resisting oppression only when you do it with love toward your adversaries. You must stand up and bear their anger without retaliation. You are a child of God, and so is every one of us. When you see God in everyone, people everywhere will begin to see God in you. True power is Universal Love.

Source: *Gandhi,* by Richard Attenborough (Video). *Gandhi the Man,* by Eknath Easwaran (Book)

MORRNAH SIMEONA
Born: 1913
Country: Hawaii (United States of America)

Why Morrnah Simeona: Morrnah was a Kahuna healing master who used *Lomi-lomi* (Hawaiian massage) to infuse her clients with profound peace and love. She adopted an ancient technique of reconciliation within island villages to harmonize anyone with anyone else any time under any circumstances. By repeating four simple phrases, spontaneous feelings of love, joy and peace can emerge. Adverse situations can be transformed. Morrnah began teaching this in the state of Hawaii, then the US and finally the entire world. American presidents came to her for healing. She even presented to the United Nations. Her work was carried on around the world by the late Dr. Ihaleakala Hew-Len, Mabel Katz, Joe Vitale, and various others.

Message: I LOVE YOU. I'M SORRY. PLEASE FORGIVE ME. THANK YOU. If you keep repeating these four simple phrases in any order, they will begin to have an uncanny and profound impact. These phrases can instill feelings of love, contrition and gratitude, key elements of prosperity. You don't need to impress others. Just repeat these words quietly within and watch what happens.

Source: *Zero Limits,* Joe Vitale (Book). *At Zero,* Joe Vitale (Book)

BILLY GRAHAM
Born: 1918
Country: United States of America

Why Billy Graham: Billy Graham directly spoke to hundreds of millions of people. For decades, Billy preached in Crusades organized by local churches all around the world. He had a unique gift of making you feel that Christ died *just for you*, that you are *the only one*, even when surrounded by 50,000 other people in a coliseum. He spoke clearly with an electrifying voice, telling stories out of local newspapers that spoke to audiences on every continent except Antarctica. Billy served as pastor and advisor to multiple U.S. presidents. His commitment to both live and preach the Gospel was nothing less than total. Billy exuded a purity that was impossible to deny. Most moving of all, Billy spoke to audiences in Communist countries, disregarding any potential political fallout. It is difficult to overestimate his impact. Next to Saint Paul, Billy Graham may have been the greatest evangelist of all time.

Message: You need Christ as the center of your life. He loves you absolutely. If you will only turn to Christ and accept Him into your heart and life, He will use you to change the world. This is the most important decision of your life. Don't delay! To avoid a Christless eternity, to avoid feeling totally lost, simply ask Him to receive you just as you are.

Source: Billy Graham, by Sarah Colt (Video)

NELSON MANDELA
Born: 1918
Country: South Africa

Why Nelson Mandela: Nelson was an activist imprisoned for his anti-apartheid organizing and political action who became one of the greatest leaders of the twentieth century. As a youthful attorney, unlike Gandhi, he advocated violence to liberate South Africa where the minority whites dictated apartheid, or extreme segregation. During that period, Nelson was implicated in a car bomb that killed nineteen people. Put away in prison for decades, Nelson transformed into something like a saint, loving even his jailors. When he left prison due to the clemency of President F.W. De Klerk, with whom he would win the Nobel Prize, his jailors mourned the loss of his company. Clint Eastwood's visionary film, *Invictus*, brilliantly depicts Nelson's ascent to the presidency, where he establishes a movement of reconciliation. The focus is on galvanizing South Africa in support of its mostly white rugby team, the Springboks. Nelson's strategy worked. The Springboks, who were performing dismally, turned everything around within a year to win the World Cup in 1995. We see whites and blacks finally hug each other, and begin to exhibit a healthy nationalism.

Message: The South African ideal of *Ubuntu* can lead us into the future. We are all one. *I cannot be me without you to define me. Nor can you be you without me to define you.* Each of us has the potential for greatness. We must think big and play big. When we combine vision with action, we have the potential for a revolution that makes a positive difference. Love, not revenge, is the most powerful weapon. With infinite patience and persistence, anything is possible.

Source: *Invictus*, by Clint Eastwood (Video)

SHIMON PERES
Born: 1923
Country: Belarus

Why Shimon Peres: As a Zionist, Shimon was one of the earliest supporters of Israel, having suffered persecution by both the Nazi Germans and the Communist Russians. He devoted his entire life to the new nation, undergoing circumstances where his country triumphed against all odds, such as the Six Day War. Early on, Shimon found himself heavily involved in arming Israel to defend itself against aggression, not only from Palestinians, but neighboring countries, as well. As Shimon grew older, he participated in a breakthrough pact, the Oslo Accords, that brought together both Israel and the Palestine Liberation Organization. He devoted his final years toward establishing lasting peace.

Message: If you want peace, you have to commit to it. You need to understand your counterpart's position without judging it. You can be both a realist and a visionary with patience. Mastering life requires substantial amounts of time. Try not to judge. Try to see what is possible. Work for its unfoldment. Faith and moral vision can triumph over all adversity.

Source: *Never Stop Dreaming: The Life and Legacy of Shimon Peres*, by Richard Trank (Video)

Marin Luther King
Born: 1929
Country: United States of America

Why Martin Luther King: Martin was a deeply spiritual, brilliant young man who earned a Ph.D. by twenty-five years of age. He was profoundly religious, convinced he must live out his faith. When Rosa Parks refused to go to the back of the bus in segregated Selma, Alabama, Rosa inadvertently prompted a movement that changed the world. Martin early on became the voice of that movement. He carefully studied the earlier movement of Mahatma Gandhi, using the same strategies, such as protests, marches, and sit-ins. As a black minister, Martin used the Bible and Christianity to appeal to the conscience of America. Martin labored for nearly a decade before ending segregation as a sanctioned legal system. His moment of glory emerged in the March on Washington on August 28, 1963, where Martin uttered his "I Have a Dream" speech, considered one of America's greatest. Martin went on to oppose the War in Vietnam, which already gave signs it would continue indefinitely. He even embraced environmentalism before it became popular. Some scholars have suggested that Martin's ultimate mission was to awaken white people. That his birthday is now a national holiday suggests that he ultimately succeeded.

Message: The Declaration of Independence guarantees the right of every American to life, liberty, and the pursuit of happiness. I have come to cash that check. I have a dream that one day this nation will rise up and live out the true meaning of its creed: We hold these truths self-evident, that all men are created equal. Injustice anywhere is a threat to justice everywhere. Love is the only force capable of transforming an enemy into friend. We are caught in an inescapable network of mutuality, tied in a single garment of destiny. Whatever affects one directly, affects all indirectly.

Source: *Selma*, by Ava DuVernay (Video)

Dalai Lama
Born: 1935
Country: Tibet

Why the Dalai Lama: The Dalai Lama has emerged from obscurity to become one of the most honored spiritual figures in history, a true spokesman for humanity. He is unique in that he has a reincarnational lineage going back centuries. The Dalai Lama is held to be the incarnation of the Bodhisattva of Compassion, *Avalokiteshvara*. Bodhisattvas refuse to enter Nirvana, or paradise, until every sentient being comes with them. As such, they might be regarded, like Christ, as world saviors. The Dalai Lama fled Tibet in his early twenties when China launched an all-out invasion of Tibet. He has a dual position as both a saint / sage and king. His office and person are vital to keeping Tibetan civilization alive. Living in exile, the Dalai Lama gradually became known worldwide, receiving the Nobel Peace Prize in 1989. He has consistently refrained from criticizing the Chinese, not only to avoid recrimination, but also because, as a Buddhist monk, he accepts that we all are responsible for our own reality. As an enthusiastic scholar of science, the Dalai Lama continually modifies his views to accommodate new discoveries. As such, he is a model of enlightenment to humanists, agnostics, and atheists the world over.

Message: My religion is kindness. We are all human. We are born, live and die. Whatever you do to someone else has a way of coming back at you. You can be of any religion, or none. Don't change your religion on account of me. Religion has its place, but we also need science. We can be both realists and optimists. We can do things with collective action that we wouldn't be able to do alone. Humanity has improved over the past centuries, despite all appearances to the contrary. The more we cultivate compassion, the more we can live in hope. Love, joy and peace are possible, not only for Buddhists, but for all of us.

Source: *Seven Years in Tibet*, by Jean-Jacques Annaud (Video)

WERNER ERHARD
Born: 1935
Country: United States of America

Why Werner Erhard: Werner Erhard, more than anyone before him, created the Transformational Movement, which has impacted every element of society, not only in America, but around the world. The psycho-spiritual methodology he developed played a vital role in bringing an end to the Cold War. Werner's courses and trainings have consistently brought clarity, responsibility and a lightness of being in communication. His two organizations, *est* and Landmark Education, have attracted many celebrities and highly influential people. People who have committed to his various programs tend to have a higher-than-average record of accomplishments. Werner's Hunger Project, heavily criticized by the media, brought critical awareness to chronic conditions, such as hunger. Although the project failed to end death by starvation, it has inspired countless initiatives to empower and enlighten humanity both individually and collectively. Through Werner's collaboration with Buckminster Fuller, world-renowned architect and theorist, he perfected the vision of a "world that works for everyone with *no one and nothing left out.*" This vision truly says it all.

Message: The world doesn't work, your lives don't work, because you continue to lie about the way it is. When you wake up to Who you truly are, you will realize that you are here to make a difference. We can predict what unconscious people will do in their mission, but we cannot predict what conscious, fully aligned people can do. Going to the moon is a perfect example of how we can make the impossible possible. At first, it seemed totally unreasonable. As we went on, the very people opposed to the massive project contributed the most to it. And finally, within a decade, humanity made its first step onto the moon. Likewise, we can continue to create a context or possibility that will alter reality as we know it.

Source: *Transformation: The Life and Legacy of Werner Erhard*, by Robyn Symon (video)

PAULA WHITE
Born: 1966
Country: United States of America

Why Paula White: Paula White illustrates what is possible for an attractive, religiously conservative woman in the twenty-first century. As a foremost televangelist and prosperity guru, Paula, as a Southern White woman, overcame a turbulent childhood with extremely modest means to develop a large charismatic church in Florida with a predominantly Black membership. Paula overcame major reversals in her life to end up personal counselor to President Donald Trump. She led the opening prayer during Trump's inauguration ceremony, and gradually became the de facto White House chaplain. If you have any impression Paula might be materialistic and shallow based on her beauty and impeccable apparel, you will be utterly shocked to follow her sermons and TV shows. She is clearly on fire for God and that love and enthusiasm is totally contagious. Paula would appear to be deeply committed to empowering and enlightening people of any color, rather than pontificating about equal rights. She enjoys high ratings from the Black community. Paula also reveals another side of President Trump that few people see. Trump has a deeply spiritual side that most people would never guess. It is no accident that Trump did everything in his power to make Jerusalem the capital of Israel.

Message: God knows you inside and out, all your weaknesses, fears, failures and doubts. God loves you with an everlasting love. He is not sitting there counting points on you. Why should He? God has infinite power at His disposal. All you need do is call on Him to begin changing your life. God is totally into empowerment. He wants you to be all you can be, regardless of your gender, race or nationality. Devote your life to God, your body, your mind, your spirit. God sees your human potential as divine possibility. You can bet your life that God will never, ever give up on you.

Source: The *Paula White* App on Apple Store and Google Play.

To save the world and fulfill the destiny of humanity requires only one thing: The Love of God. God IS Love, and Love IS God. The Lord of the Universe is incarnate in the Lord of Love, God made visible. As God has been made visible in Jesus Christ, and every other avatar, bodhisattva and messiah of pure Love, so also can God be made visible in you and in each of us. The truth is, as God IS Love, so are you. Let's join together and create the one moonshot that ultimately counts. Not just another fancy rocket, a you and me world, a world that works for everyone with no one and nothing left out.

Thank you for joining me this far. I know it won't be long before we all embrace. God bless you forever with His Infinite, Absolute and Universal Love.

Structured Prayer

(From the Christian Tradition by Phil Brattain)

The following prayer is a silent meditation developed over the better part of twenty years. It is between God and me. In it, I pray for both people and countries. I use simple words, such as "bless," "forgive," and "heal." I address the God of my childhood faith in a whole new way. I view the center of that faith being the Lord of LOVE, Jesus Christ. Since Christ is seen to be THE Son of God, I recognize His Love, that LOVE, to be the express image of the Invisible God. As we commune with that LOVE, we become, step by step, stage by stage, Christ, the new humanity/divinity. We become THIS VERY LOVE.

This endeavor has led me to Universalism, all faiths, all traditions, and to being a Christian Hindu. I find myself deeply resonating to the intersection of two of our Great Faiths. My deep study of Hinduism has led me to become more of a Christian than I ever imagined possible. Finally, I am a mystical Christian. Mystics in any tradition are not satisfied with anything less than the ultimate.

This morning prayer follows systematic study of the holy scriptures of every tradition, including the Christian. I then make four yogic breaths and with closed eyes say:

[*Last words of the Hindu Saint, Neem Karola Baba.*]
All Hail the Lord of the Universe!
All Hail the Lord of the Universe!

All Hail the Lord of the Universe!

[*Invocation to Jesus the Chosen One, the Lord of LOVE.*]
Meshiya Yeshua.
Meshiya Yeshua.
Meshiya Yeshua.

[*Invocation to the Great I AM, Our Father, Our Source, Our God.*]
Yah-Weh *(Breathed)*
Yah-Weh *(Breathed)*
Yah-Weh *(Breathed)*

Come Lord Jesus, dawn in the heart of every sentient being!

Thank you for the gift of Eternal Life. Thank you for the underlying reality of ABSOLUTE UNITY, ABSOLUTE LOVE, and ABSOLUTE PERFECTION.

God bless America! Bless our president. Bless our vice president. May they both be all they can possibly be in this life. May they become the highest possible version of themselves.

Bless Israel, Palestine, and Lebanon. Bless your Holy Land.
Bless Pakistan, India, and Bangladesh.
Bless Sri Lanka, Nepal, and Tibet.
Bless China, Japan, North Korea, and South Korea.

Bless Russia. Bless its president. Bless his family, his community, and his country. May he find true happiness. May he wake up to the infinite power of your LOVE. Forgive Russia for attacking Ukraine. Make him a blessing, and not a curse, to all his neighbors and to every country.

Bless the Ukraine. Bless its president. Grant him the power, grace, and courage to bring an end to the violence in his country. Heal the deep wounds the recent war has created.

May both Russia and Ukraine come together once again as brother and sister.

May true leadership emerge all over our planet, in every country, city, village, and community.

Praise be to the Lord of Light, the Lord of Life, the Lord of Love! Glory be to God in the highest!
May we all awaken into Universal Consciousness, Universal Love, Universal Presence!

Your LOVE is the most powerful force in all the Universe. Make us agents of that LOVE wherever we go to whomever we meet.

Bless the great congregation of all humanity, past, present, and future! Bring us all back together again.

Come home, Meshiya Yeshua, to your planet and our planet, to your people and our people.

I encourage you to create your own structured prayer. Honor the deepest sentiments of your heart. Invoke God in the form that most profoundly speaks to you. Regard Him or Her as your best friend, your ultimate Lover. You can thereby speak in the most intimate fashion. This is YOUR prayer. It is a two-way conversation. Even more, it is Sacred Communion.

Resources to Get Started

[B] = Book, [A] = Audio, [V] = Video, [O] = Organization

Attenborough, Richard
Gandhi [V], Sony Pictures, 2007.

Barks, Coleman
The Illuminated Rumi [B] with Michael Green, Broadway Books, 1997.
One Song: A New Illuminated Rumi, Running Press, Illustrated Edition, 2005.

Campbell, Joseph
The Power of Myth [V], 25th Anniversary Edition, Athena Video, 2013.

Chopra, Deepak
Power, Freedom and Grace [B], Amber-Allen Publishing, 2008.
The Third Jesus [B], Harmony, 2009

Easwaran, Eknath
Gandhi The Man: The Story of His Transformation [B], Nilgiri Press, 2007.
The Dhammapada: A Classic of Indian Spirituality [B], Nilgigi Press, 2007.
The Upanishads: A Classic of Indian Spirituality [B], Nilgiri Press, 2007.
The Bhagavad Gita: A Classic of Indian Spirituality [B], Nilgiri Press, 2007.
God Makes the Rivers to Flow: An Anthology of the World's Sacred Poetry and Prose, Nilgiri Press, 2009.

Eddy, Mary Baker
Science and Health with Key to the Scriptures [B], Authorized Trade Edition, The Christian Science Board of Directors, 2000.

Eliot, T.S.
Four Quartets [B], Ecco: First Edition, 2023.

Fox, Mathew
Meditations with Meister Eckhart [B], Bear & Company, 1983.
Meister Eckhart: A Mystic Warrior for Our Times [B], New World Library, 2014.

Hixon, Lex
Great Swan: Meetings with Ramakrishna, [B], Larson Publications, 1997.

Holy Bible, New King James Version, (B), Thomas Nelson, 2018.

Kaufman, Philip
The Right Stuff (Two-Disc Speical Edition) [V], Warner Home Video, 2003.

Ladinsky, Daniel
The Gift: Poems by Hafiz, The Great Sufi Master [B], Penguin Compass, 2002.
Love Poems from God: Twelve Sacred Voices from the East and West [B], Penguin Compass, 2002.
The Subject Tonight Is Love: 60 Wild and Sweet Poems of Hafiz [B], Penguin Compass, 2003.

Landmark Education [O] (www.landmarkworldwide.com)
The Forum
The Communication Course: Access to Power
The Advanced Communication Course: The Power to Create

Maharaj, Nisargadatta
I Am That: Talks with Sri Nisargadatta Maharaj [B], Chetana Private Ltd., 1989.

Maharshi, Ramana
The Spiritual Teachings [B], Shambala Classics, 1998.
The Essential Teachings of Ramana Maharshi: A Visual Journey [B], Inner Directions, 2002.

MindValley.com [O]
Courses by Vishen Lakhiani, especially *Be Extraordinary*.

Neruda, Pablo and Mitchell, Stephen
Full Woman, Fleshly Apple, Hot Moon: Selected Poems of Pablo Neruda [B], Harper Perennial Modern Classics, 2009.

Pearson, Carlton
The Gospel of Inclusion: Reaching Beyond Religious Fundamentalism [B], Atria, 2009.

Peterson, Eugene H.
The Message Remix: The Bible in Contemporary Language [B], NavPress, First Thus Edition, 2019.

Ram Dass, Baba
Remember Be Here Now [B], Hanuman Foundation, 1971.
Miracle of Love: Stories About Neem Karoli Baba [B], Hanuman Foundation, 1995.

Ray, Nicholas
King of Kings [V], Warner Home Video, 2011.

Rinehart, Luke
The Book of est [B], Lulu.com, 2010

Rohr, Richard
The Divine Dance: The Trinity and Your Transformation [B] Whitaker House, 2020.
The Universal Christ: How a Forgotten Reality Can Change Everything, [B], Convergent Books, 2021.

Science and Nonduality (*www.scienceandnonduality.com*) [O]

Silent Unity (www.unity.org) [O]

Smith, Huston
The Illustrated World's Religions: A Guide to Our Wisdom Traditions [B], HarperOne, 1995.

The Beatles
Yellow Submarine [V], MGM, 1999.

Twyman, James
The Prayer of Saint Francis [B], Findhorn Press, 2002.

Tzu, Lao
Tao Te Ching: A New English Version [B], Stephen Mitchell, Perennial Classics, 2006.
The Second Book of the Tao [B], Stephen Mitchell, Penguin Books, 2010.

Wachowski, Larry and Andy
The Matrix Trilogy [V] Warner Home Video, Blu-ray, 2007.

Watts, Alan

Out of Your Mind: Essential Listening [A], Sounds True, 2005.

Do You Do It or Does It Do You? How to Let the Universe Meditate [A], Sounds True, 2005.

You're It!: On Hiding: Seeking and Being Found [A], Sounds True, 2009.

Myth and Ritual in Christianity [B], Beacon Press, 1971.

Behold the Spirit: A Study in the Necessity of Religion [B], Vintage, Revised Edition, 1972.

The Two Hands of God: The Myths of Polarity, [B] New World Library, 2020 .

Beyond Theology: The Art of Godmanship, New World Library [B], 2022.

Wilber, Ken

The Integral Vision: A Very Short Introduction [B], Shambhala, 2007.

Acknowledgments

Thought Leaders:

Theology: My vision of God has been profoundly shaped by **Richard Rohr, Matthew Fox, Carlton Pearson, Neale Donald Walsch, T.S. Eliot, Mary Baker Eddy,** and **Dame Julian of Norwich.**

Comparative Religion: I have progressively opened up to the wisdom of the world's spiritual traditions thanks to **Huston Smith, Alan Watts,** and **Joseph Campbell,** as well as the incomparable Sufi poets **Hafez** and **Rumi.**

Enlightenment: The scholars **Lex Hixon** and **Eknath Easwaran** have been indispensable to my arriving at a breakthrough perspective.

Transformation: My deepest debt may be to those who turned me upside down: **Werner Erhard, Bucky Fuller, Deepak Chopra, Andrew Cohen, Ken Wilber, Otto Scharmer, Paula White, Billy Graham,** and **Mahatma Gandhi.**

New Paradigm: My vision of reality *and what is possible* have been forever turned inside out thanks to **Fritjof Capra, Amit Goswamy, Michio Kaku, Brian Greene, John Hagelin, Steve Jobs, Maurizio and Zaya Benazzi, Peter Diamandis,** and **Ray Kurzweil.**

Blessing: I live in the spirit in a way I would never have even imagined thanks to the work of **Morrnah Simeona, Dr. Ihaleakala Hew-Len, Joe Vitale,** and **Mata Amritanandamayi.**

Prosperity: I have been shown the way to practical abundance step by step thanks to the incomparable vision, passion, and courage of **Tony Robbins, Rhonda Byrne, Bob Proctor, Jack Canfield,** and **Napoleon Hill.**

Primary Support:

Inner Circle: I owe a lifetime of thanks to **Audrone Wippich, Suresh Narayanan, Janice Peterson, G.S. Satya, Sheridan Tatsuno, Arjuna Noor, Christina Cheney, Olivier Minkowski, Jane Brattain, Col. James Brattain, Hans Heimburger, Majeed Shekarchi,** and **Mark Koo.** These people have been with me in so many ways for so many years, never withholding their active love and guidance.

Hollywood: I wouldn't have been able to even think of knocking on the door without the ceaseless patience and good humor of **Scott Ross, Sandy Climan, Theodore Garcia, Sydney iWanter, Alex Barder, Thomas Trenker, Sergio Toglatti, Robin Rowe, Brad Nye, Pat Krishnan, Art Cohen,** and **Tom Schlesinger.**

Entrepreneurialism: My efforts to serve and support the brilliant technologists in Silicon Valley were possibly only through the grace of such dedicated professionals as **Mukul Agarwal, Venkat Bhat, Srikanth Erode, Raghu Holla, Vish Mishra, Cameron Nazeri, Joe Neil Zelaya, Thomas Varghese,** and **Ganesh Mandalam.**

First Readers:

Much thanks to those courageous luminaries who gave up considerable time to review my manuscript in its early stages, including **Landon Carter, Olivier Minkowski, Michael Bishop, Nick Brown, Michael David Lee, Cristina Smith,** and **Steven Harrison,** along with **Jack Canfield.**

Publishing:

I am in a solid position to publish this manuscript only because of such true professionals as **Ann McIndoo, Steve Harrison, Jack Canfield, Geoffrey Berwind, Cristina Smith, Valerie Costa, Christy Day, and John Kremer.**

About the Author

PHIL BRATTAIN co-authored *Awaken Perfection: The Journey of Conscious Revelation* with Audrone Wippich, winning endorsements from Dr. Arun Gandhi, grandson of the Mahatma, and Tenzin N. Tethong, president of the Dalai Lama Foundation. He then joined Audrone to write 200 articles for *Conscious Owl*, a web magazine focused on global and contemporary spirituality. Having researched the great spiritual and mystical traditions over twenty years, Phil has been active in the interfaith movement. He developed a firm conviction that *the very heart of religion is Divine, or Universal, Love. If people get this right, everything else worthwhile will follow.*

Having lived most of his life in Northern California, Phil has been deeply influenced by a culture of continuous innovation preoccupied with reinventing the future. He has developed extensive friendships with international engineers and entrepreneurs, gaining a global perspective on social, political, and environmental issues. In the process, Phil developed a lasting relationship with the South Asia diaspora. He started out as a technical recruiter and executive search consultant, leading to global business development for ventures seeking to enter the North American market through San Francisco's Silicon Valley. In building out client portfolios, Phil has befriended executives across the United States. Recently, he has led several initiatives into Hollywood, promoting cutting-edge big data, blockchain, and A.I.

Phil Brattain earned a B.A. from the University of California, Berkeley, in Cultural and Intellectual History with strong minors in French and English. He subsequently discovered the human potential and transformational movements, participating in encounter groups, seminars, symposia, and conferences. Phil has been active with Landmark Education, MindValley, and Science and Nonduality. He practices Christian Science among other disciplines. Phil is also active in such entrepreneurial groups as TiE, Angel Launch, and BootUP World, where he mentors startups, helping them go to market and establish key reference accounts for further capitalization. When he can, Phil likes to escape to the nearby resort of Carmel by the Sea, where he roams the art galleries and relishes the fine European cuisine in a forest overlooking the Pacific Ocean. He also frequently joins close friends in Hawaii to keep the spirit of *Aloha* alive.

GET YOUR FREE DOWNLOADABLE GUIDE

How to Presence Universal Love in Your Life and Your World... Starting Today

www.Waging.Love

You are invited to join what could be the greatest movement of our time: *The Moonshot of Universal Love.* Help empower one billion of us with direct access to this LOVE, and the ability to channel that LOVE to anyone, anywhere, anytime and in any circumstances.

Divine, Unconditional, All-Embracing LOVE is the most powerful force in all the Universe. With It, you find that God IS Love, and so are you, and so are all of us.